US CITIZENSHIP STUDY GUIDE

A Complete Guidebook Equipping Immigrants with the Knowledge, Tools, and Confidence to Navigate the Naturalization Process, Ace the Citizenship Exam, and Embrace Their New Citizenship Status

THEODORE WRIGHT

TABLE OF CONTENTS

Introduction to US Naturalization/Citizenship Test

Becoming a citizen of the USA is a momentous and life-changing step that many individuals aspire to take. The naturalization process, which includes the US citizenship test, is designed to ensure that those seeking citizenship possess a fundamental understanding of the nation's history, government, and civic responsibilities. This comprehensive guide aims to demystify the process in navigating the journey to becoming a US citizen.

Overview of the Test and Naturalization Process

Embarking on the journey to attain US citizenship through naturalization is a substantial endeavor, encompassing a detailed process operated by the USCIS. The anticipated processing duration typically ranges from 18 to 24 months, though it can vary depending on factors such as the applicant's location, USCIS workload, and the precision of the application submission.

1. Investigation and Eligibility Assessment

The journey to US citizenship begins with an investigation conducted by the USCIS. The primary objective of this phase is to assess an individual's eligibility for naturalization. Several factors contribute to this assessment:

- **Lawful Permanent Residency (Green Card):** To be eligible for naturalization, a green card, also known as lawful permanent residency, is required for an applicant to satisfy the requirements. They have the permission to live and work in the US indefinitely. Green card holders are those who have green cards.

- **Continuous Residence:** Continuous residence is a crucial criterion, requiring applicants to maintain a permanent home in the United States. Brief trips abroad are generally allowed, but extended absences may impact an applicant's eligibility.

- **Physical Presence:** In addition to continuous residence, there is a requirement for physical presence in the US. This entails spending a specific period of time within the country during the qualifying period.

- **Good Moral Character:** Applicants are expected to demonstrate good moral character, adhering to US laws and embodying ethical behavior. Criminal convictions, tax evasion, and other factors may be considered in the assessment of an individual's moral character.

2. Application Submission

Once the investigation phase is completed, eligible individuals can proceed to the next step by submitting Form N-400, the Application for Naturalization. This form serves as a comprehensive document, capturing essential information about the applicant's background, residence, and other pertinent details. It is crucial to fill out this form accurately and truthfully, as any discrepancies may impact the naturalization process.

3. Biometrics Appointment

After submitting the application, applicants are required to attend a biometrics appointment. During this session, fingerprints are taken for identification and security purposes. Biometrics play a vital role in verifying the identity of the applicant and ensuring the accuracy of the information provided in the application.

4. Interview and Civics Test

The heart of the naturalization process lies in the interview, during which an USCIS officer reviews the N-400 application with the applicant. This interview serves multiple purposes:

- **English Language Proficiency Test:** The officer assesses the applicant's ability to speak, read, and write in English. Effective communication in English is a fundamental aspect of becoming a US citizen, and the interview provides an opportunity to evaluate this proficiency.

- **Civics Test:** The applicant's understanding of the history and governance of the United States is evaluated through the civics test. It consists of questions related to the Constitution, the Bill of Rights, the branches of government, and other essential civic topics. Applicants must answer a set number of questions correctly to demonstrate their understanding.

5. English Language Proficiency Test

In addition to the English language assessment during the interview, there is a standalone English language proficiency test. This test ensures that applicants possess the necessary language skills to communicate effectively in English, a crucial requirement for active participation in American society.

6. Oath of Allegiance

Upon successfully completing the interview and tests, eligible applicants proceed to a naturalization ceremony. As part of this solemn ceremony, prospective members of the

US swear the Oath of Allegiance, which is a symbolic vow that affirms their devotion to the founding principles and ideals of the US. The individual's official position as a citizen of the USA is signaled by the taking of this oath, which symbolizes the culmination of the naturalization process.

Eligibility and Requirements for Applying

Becoming a US citizen through the naturalization process requires meeting specific eligibility criteria, particularly related to residence and moral character. Understanding these requirements is critical for aspiring citizens to navigate the path to US citizenship successfully.

1. Age Requirement

One of the fundamental eligibility criteria for US naturalization is age. Applicants must be almost 18 years old at the time of filing Form N-400, the Application for Naturalization. This requirement ensures that individuals seeking citizenship have reached the age of majority and are legally capable of making independent decisions.

2. Lawful Permanent Residency (Green Card)

Possessing lawful permanent residency, commonly known as a green card, is a cornerstone of eligibility for naturalization. Green card holders are individuals who have been granted the right to live and work in the US permanently. The general requirement is that an applicant must have held a green card for a continuous period of five years. However, there is an exclusion for spouses of US citizens, who may be eligible after three years of permanent residency if certain criteria are met.

3. Continuous Residence

Continuous residence is a critical component of eligibility and pertains to an applicant's ability to maintain a permanent home in the United States. This requirement ensures that individuals seeking citizenship have a sustained connection to the country. While brief trips abroad are generally allowed, extended absences may disrupt the continuous residence requirement and impact an applicant's eligibility.

4. Physical Presence

In addition to continuous residence, there is a requirement for physical presence within the United States. This means that applicants must have spent a specific amount of time within the country during the qualifying period. The aim is to demonstrate a commitment to being an active part of the US community and engaging in the daily life of the nation.

5. Good Moral Character

One of the most fundamental requirements for naturalization in the United States is the demonstration of a decent moral character. This includes abiding by the laws of the United

States, and paying taxes, while not engaging in illegal actions. USCIS may consider a range of factors when assessing an applicant's moral character, including arrests, convictions, and overall behavior. This requirement emphasizes the importance of ethical conduct in the naturalization process.

6. English Language Proficiency

The capacity to speak, read, and write in English is a crucial component of US naturalization. During the interview, an USCIS officer assesses the applicant's English language proficiency. Effective communication in English is fundamental to active participation in American society, and this requirement ensures that new citizens can engage meaningfully with their communities.

7. Civics Knowledge

Applicants must demonstrate knowledge of US government and history through the civics test. This test is an integral part of the naturalization process and covers essential topics such as the Constitution, the Bill of Rights, and the functions of the branches of government. Obtaining a score that is satisfactory on the civics examination is necessary in order to satisfy the civics knowledge criterion.

8. Attachment to the Constitution

Applicants are expected to make a declaration that they are committed to the values and principles outlined in the Constitution of the United States. Furthermore, they are required to declare that they are prepared to use their arms in support of the USA or to serve in the Armed Forces in a capacity that does not include combat. This requirement underscores the commitment expected from those seeking US citizenship.

9. Oath of Allegiance

One of the final steps in the naturalization process is the Oath of Allegiance. During the naturalization ceremony, applicants take this solemn oath, pledging allegiance to the US and renouncing allegiance to any foreign country. The Oath of Allegiance is a symbolic and profound moment, marking the culmination of the naturalization journey.

Exceptions for Disabled Individuals

Recognizing the diverse needs of applicants, USCIS has implemented exceptions and accommodations for individuals with disabilities. These exceptions aim to ensure that the naturalization process is accessible to all, regardless of physical or developmental challenges.

- **Accommodations during the Interview and Tests:** Disabled individuals may request accommodations during the naturalization interview and tests. These accommodations may include modified test questions, additional time, or the use of assistive devices.

The goal is to create an inclusive environment that allows individuals with disabilities to demonstrate their eligibility for US citizenship effectively.

- **Waiver of English Language Proficiency and Civics Test:** In some cases, individuals with disabilities may be eligible for a waiver of the English language proficiency and civics test requirements. This waiver acknowledges that certain medical conditions may impact an individual's ability to meet these specific requirements. However, the waiver is not automatic and requires a formal request, supported by appropriate documentation from a medical professional.

Exceptions for Seniors

Seniors, individuals aged 50 or older at the time of filing for naturalization and having been lawful permanent residents for at least 20 years, or individuals aged 55 or older with at least 15 years of lawful permanent residency, may be eligible for certain exceptions.

- **English Language Proficiency Test Exemption:** The English language competency test may not be required of senior applicants who not only meet the age requirement but also meet the residency requirements. This recognizes that language acquisition may become more challenging with age, and the exemption allows seniors to demonstrate their civic knowledge without the added language requirement.

- **Civics Test in Native Language:** While the general expectation is that the civics test is conducted in English, seniors meeting the age and residency criteria have the option to take the civics test in their native language. This exception acknowledges the cultural and linguistic diversity of older applicants.

We are dedicated to crafting high-quality products and strive to ensure maximum customer satisfaction. We would be deeply grateful if you could contribute to our growth.

*Once you have finished reading the book, **your review would be immensely valuable to us**.*
Thank you from the bottom of our hearts!

Mastering the English Test: A Comprehensive Strategy

CHAPTER

2

Mastering the English Language Test is a fundamental step for individuals aspiring to become US citizens. This segment assesses basic proficiency in writing, reading, and speaking English. It's essential to note that this is not a professional English test, and applicants need not have a flawless command of the language or an American accent to be considered eligible. This chapter delves into the three components of the English Language Test: Speaking, Reading, and Writing.

Speaking Test: Here's How It Goes

The Speaking Test is designed to evaluate the applicant's understanding of the English language. A designated USCIS officer engages the applicant in a conversation, posing a series of questions. The applicant's speaking ability is gauged based on the accuracy of both grammar and content in their responses.

Procedure:

- The USCIS officer poses questions, ensuring clarity and simplicity.

- If the applicant struggles to comprehend a question, the officer may repeat or rephrase it to facilitate understanding.

- In the event of persistent difficulty in answering, the officer assesses that the applicant may not have a complete understanding of the English language.

Passing Criteria:

- The applicant succeeds if they demonstrate comprehension of questions and provide satisfactory responses.

- In case of unsatisfactory answers, the applicant fails this portion but remains eligible for the remaining sections of the test.

Reading Test: Here's How It Goes

The Reading Test is designed to evaluate the applicant's capacity to read sentences written in English syntax. The candidate is presented with a maximum of three sentences and must accurately read at least one of them. The focus is on conveying meaning, allowing for minor errors in pronunciation.

Criteria for Failure:

- The applicant fails the test if unable to correctly read at least one sentence.

- Extreme pronunciation errors leading to a significant change in sentence meaning result in failure.

- Prolonged pauses between words or the omission of words altering the sentence's meaning lead to failure.

Vocabulary List

1. **People:** Abraham Lincoln, George Washington

2. **Civics:** American flag, Bill of Rights, capital, citizen, city, Congress, country, Father of Our Country, government, President, right, Senators, state/states, White House.

3. **Places:** America, United States, US

4. **Holidays:** Presidents' Day, Memorial Day, Flag Day, Independence Day, Labor Day, Columbus Day, Thanksgiving

5. **Question Words:** How, What, When, Where, Who, Why

6. **Verbs:** Can, come, do/does, elects, have/has, is/are/was/be, lives/lived, meet, name, pay, vote, want

7. **Other (function):** a, for, here, in, of, on, the, to we

8. **Other (content):** colors, dollar bill, first, largest, many, most, north, one, people, second, south

Writing Test: Here's How It Goes

Similar to the Reading Test, the Writing Test evaluates the applicant's capacity to convey meaning in written English. The USCIS officer orally dictates a sentence, and the applicant must write it in a manner comprehensible to the officer. The emphasis is on basic understanding rather than professional proficiency in grammar, punctuation, or spelling.

Passing Criteria:

- The test concludes when the applicant successfully writes a sentence understandable to the officer.

- Permissible mistakes include grammatical, punctuation, or spelling errors that do not compromise the sentence's meaning.

- Omission of non-essential words or the use of digits instead of English spellings is acceptable.

Failure Criteria:

- Failure occurs when the applicant cannot convey the intended meaning in their written sentence.

- Complete alteration of the sentence or word, usage of short forms, or construction of a sentence lacking coherence results in failure.

Vocabulary List

1. **People:** Adams; Lincoln, Washington

2. **Civics:** American Indians, capital, citizens, civil war, congress, Father of Our Country, flag, free, freedom of speech, President, right, Senators, state/states, White House

3. **Places:** Alaska, California, Canada, Delaware, Mexico, New York City, United States, Washington, Washington D.C.

4. **Months:** February, May, June, July, September, October, November

5. **Holidays:** Presidents' Day, Memorial Day, Flag Day, Independence Day, Labor Day, Columbus Day, Thanksgiving.

6. **Verbs:** Can, come, elect, have/has, is/was/be, lives/lived, meets, pay, vote, want

7. **Other (function):** and, during, for, here, in, of, on, the, to, we.

8. **Other (content):** blue, dollar bill, fifty/50, first, largest, most, north, one, one hundred/100, people, red, second, south, taxes, white.

CHAPTER

The Civics Test Explained
Structure of the Civics Test

3

In this comprehensive chapter, we delve into an in-depth exploration of the structure of the Civics Test, a pivotal component of the journey towards US citizenship. The chapter is strategically divided into three main sections, each focusing on distinct aspects of American governance and history, as well as integrated civics components.

American Government

The USA, often referred to as the "land of the free," is a nation built on a unique foundation of democratic principles, a carefully designed system of government, and a set of rights and responsibilities that define the relationship between citizens and the state.

Principles of American Democracy

- **Popular Sovereignty**

The concept of popular power is the fundamental tenet of democratic government in the US, a concept rooted in Enlightenment philosophy and deeply embedded in the nation's history. Popular sovereignty asserts that ultimate governmental authority resides with the people. By exercising their right to vote, residents are given the ability to take an active role in the process of democracy, which is an ever-changing force that enables citizens to do so. The revolutionary concept that the authority of government originates from the approval of the people who are governed is reflected in this foundational principle.

The historical roots of popular sovereignty can be traced back to key Enlightenment thinkers like John Locke, whose ideas greatly influenced the framers of the US Constitution. The Constitution itself, with its emphasis on "We the People," encapsulates the essence of popular sovereignty, serving as a testament to the democratic ideals that inspired the birth of the nation.

In practice, popular sovereignty manifests during elections, where citizens exercise their right to vote to choose their representatives. This participation is not just a civic duty but a fundamental aspect of shaping the direction and policies of the government.

• Rule of Law

In the context of the legal system, the idea of the rule of law is a fundamental notion that emphasizes the equal status of everyone before the judge. It emphasizes that no one, including government officials, is above the law. This principle ensures the existence of a just and fair legal system where decisions are made based on established laws and principles rather than arbitrary or discriminatory factors.

The historical roots of the rule of law can be traced to the Magna Carta and further developed by thinkers such as Montesquieu during the Enlightenment. The Founding Fathers incorporated the rule of law into the US Constitution as a safeguard against tyranny, establishing a legal framework that governs the behavior of both citizens and government officials.

In practice, the rule of law provides a foundation for individual rights and liberties, ensuring due process, protection against unjust actions, and maintaining the integrity of the legal system. It is a cornerstone of American democracy, contributing to the nation's reputation for upholding justice and the rights of its citizens.

• Individual Rights

Through the Bill of Rights and later modifications to the Constitution, the preservation of individual liberties is a distinguishing characteristic of the democratic system that exists in the USA. These rights encompass a broad spectrum of freedoms, including freedom of speech, religion, and assembly, ensuring that individuals have the autonomy to express themselves and actively participate in civic life.

The historical roots of individual rights can be traced to the struggles of the American colonists against British rule. The grievances expressed in documents like the Declaration of Independence underscored the importance of safeguarding individual liberties. The Bill of Rights, added to the Constitution shortly after its ratification, was a response to the need for explicit protections of these fundamental rights.

In practice, individual rights provide citizens with the tools to challenge the government, express dissent, and contribute to the diverse tapestry of American society. These rights are not static; they adapt and evolve to address contemporary challenges and changing societal norms.

- ## Checks and Balances

The notion of checks and balances is a complex process that is ingrained in the government structure of the USA. Its purpose is to avoid the accumulation of power in any one of the branches of government. This concept acknowledges the potential for abuses of power and seeks to distribute authority among the legislative, executive, and judicial branches, creating a system of mutual oversight.

The intellectual origins of checks and balances can be traced to Enlightenment thinkers like Montesquieu, whose ideas greatly influenced the framers of the US Constitution. The Constitution's establishment of separate and distinct branches of government reflects a deliberate effort to ensure accountability and prevent the emergence of tyranny.

In practice, the checks and balances system necessitates cooperation and negotiation among the branches. The legislative branch is responsible for drafting laws, the executive branch is responsible for enforcing those laws, and the judicial branch is responsible for interpreting those laws. Each arm of government is vested with the authority to monitor and control the activities of the other branches, so establishing an unstable balance that prevents the misuse of power.

System of Government

- ## Federalism

The concept of federalism is a key feature of the US system of government, delineating the distribution of powers between the national government and individual states. This dual system allows states to address local concerns while the federal government oversees matters of national importance.

The historical roots of federalism can be traced to the compromises made during the Constitutional Convention. The concept of federalism originated as a solution to the problem of striking a balance between the necessity for a powerful central authority and the desire to maintain the independence of various states. It is important to note that the Tenth Amendment emphasizes the notion of limited government by specifically reserving responsibilities that have not been assigned to the federal government to the states.

In practice, federalism manifests in a diverse range of policies and laws across the country. States have the authority to govern aspects such as education, criminal law, and public health, contributing to a rich tapestry of legal and policy landscapes. The balance between federal and state powers remains a dynamic aspect of American governance, subject to ongoing debates and legal interpretations.

• Separation of Powers

Legislative, executive, and judicial departments of government are each established by the Constitution of the USA as distinct and independent branches of government, all having their own set of authorities and obligations. The resulting division of powers helps to ensure that no single branch of government rises to an excessively dominant position, which in turn helps to prevent abuses of authority and promote accountability.

The historical roots of the separation of powers can be traced to Enlightenment thinkers like John Locke and Baron de Montesquieu. The framers of the Constitution were deeply influenced by these ideas, seeking to create a government structure that would prevent the concentration of power and protect against potential abuses.

From a practical standpoint, the division of powers guarantees that each branch of government functions independently, with distinct duties and obligations respectively. The formation of legislation falls under the purview of the legislative branch, which is governed by Congress. It is the responsibility of the executive branch, which is led by the President, to ensure that laws are followed. When it comes to implementing legislation, the responsibility falls on the judicial branch, which is headed by the federal courts. This distribution of powers fosters a system where each branch can act as a check on the others, promoting a balanced and accountable government.

• Democratic Governance

A democracy with representation is the kind of government that is used in the USA. In this system, individuals elect delegates for making choices on their behalf. The implementation of this idea guarantees that the government will continue to be attentive to the will of the people, reflecting the foundational principle that government derives its legitimacy from the consent of the governed.

The historical roots of democratic governance can be traced to the drafting of the US Constitution, where the framers sought to establish a government that reflected the democratic ideals born out of the American Revolution. The Constitution's provisions for regular elections, the separation of powers, and individual rights collectively contribute to a system that values and incorporates democratic principles.

In practice, democratic governance involves the electoral process, political parties, and civic participation. Citizens have the opportunity to engage in the democratic process through voting, running for office, and participating in grassroots movements. This active involvement is not only a right but also a responsibility, reinforcing the reciprocal nature of the relationship between the government and its citizens.

Rights and Responsibilities

Rights of US Citizens

- **Freedom of Speech:** The right to freedom of speech is protected by the First Amendment, which enables individuals to freely convey their thoughts, ideas, and beliefs without the fear of being censored under any circumstances.

- **Freedom of Religion:** The freedom of religion is another aspect that is safeguarded by the First Amendment. This ensures that individuals are able to follow what they believe or decide not to subscribe to any religious views.

- **Right to Bear Arms:** The Second Amendment grants citizens the right to bear arms, reflecting historical and constitutional considerations related to self-defense and the security of a free state.

- **Right to a Fair Trial:** The Constitution guarantees the right to a fair and speedy trial, emphasizing due process and protection against unjust legal proceedings.

- **Right to Vote:** The right to vote is a fundamental aspect of democratic citizenship, providing individuals with a direct means to influence government policies and representation.

Responsibilities of US Citizens

- **Voting in Elections:** Actively participating in the electoral process by voting in local, state, and federal elections is a fundamental obligation of US citizens. Voting is not only a right but also a civic duty that contributes to the functioning of a representative democracy.

- **Serving on a Jury:** When called upon, citizens have the obligation to serve on a jury, participating in the legal system and ensuring that justice is administered fairly.

- **Respecting the Rights of Others:** Citizenship involves respecting the rights and beliefs of others, fostering a diverse and inclusive society where individuals with varying perspectives can coexist harmoniously.

- **Staying Informed and Engaged:** Citizens are encouraged to stay informed about political issues, government policies, and current events. Informed citizens are better equipped to make meaningful contributions to civic discourse and advocate for their interests.

American History

Colonial Period and Independence

The foundations of American history are firmly rooted in the colonial period, a time of exploration, settlement, and the gradual forging of a unique identity. Christopher Columbus's historic journey in 1492 revealed the existence of the American continent to the world, setting the stage for a transformative chapter in global history.

Prior to European colonization, the vast and varied landscapes of America were home to diverse Native American populations, each with its distinct cultures, languages, and ways of life. The arrival of European explorers initiated a complex and often tumultuous interaction between these established societies and the newcomers.

The 13 colonies, scattered along the eastern seaboard, emerged as focal points of European settlement. Each colony, with its peculiarities and contributions, played a crucial role in shaping the American narrative. The list of the 13 colonies reads like a roster of the early architects of the nation: Massachusetts, Pennsylvania, Rhode Island, New Hampshire, Connecticut, New York, New Jersey, Virginia, Delaware, North Carolina, South Carolina, Georgia, and Maryland.

Colonists embarked on this journey for diverse reasons, ranging from religious freedom to economic opportunities. The character of each colony was shaped by its founding principles, economic pursuits, and the interplay of cultures. However, the harmonious pursuit of liberty was disrupted by tensions with the British Crown. Heavy taxation, lack of self-government, and the presence of British soldiers in American homes created a powder keg of dissent.

The culmination of these tensions was the adoption of the Declaration of Independence on July 4, 1776. Authored primarily by Thomas Jefferson, this revolutionary document articulated the colonies' grievances, proclaimed their inherent rights, and declared their intent to sever ties with British rule. The ensuing American Revolutionary War tested the resolve of the fledgling nation and ultimately resulted in victory, securing the United States' independence.

Creation and Adoption of the Constitution

The aftermath of the Revolutionary War brought the newly independent states face to face with the challenges of governance. The Articles of Confederation, the initial attempt at a national constitution, revealed weaknesses that necessitated a reevaluation. The Constitutional Convention of 1787, held in Philadelphia, marked a critical juncture where the Founding Fathers gathered to draft a more robust and enduring constitution.

The resulting US Constitution laid the groundwork for the federal system, emphasizing a delicate balance between the central government and individual states. The principles of separation of powers and checks and balances became guiding tenets, designed to prevent the concentration of authority and safeguard individual liberties. The Federalists, led by figures like James Madison and Alexander Hamilton, championed the Constitution as a means to create a strong central government, fostering effective interstate relations.

On the opposing side were the Anti-Federalists, who feared the potential tyranny of a powerful central authority. Their concerns led to the addition of the Bill of Rights, the first ten amendments to the Constitution, which explicitly protected individual freedoms. George Washington's leadership, both on the battlefield during the Revolutionary War and as the first President of the United States, solidified his place as the "Father of Our Country" and a key figure in the nation's formative years.

The 1800s

The 19th century unfolded as an era of territorial expansion, conflicts, and the crystallization of a distinct American identity. The Louisiana Purchase in 1803, orchestrated by President Thomas Jefferson, was a transformative acquisition, doubling the size of the nation and opening new frontiers for exploration and settlement.

However, the century was also marked by internal strife, none more defining than the American Civil War (1861-1865). This conflict, rooted in profound divisions, particularly over slavery, pitted the Northern states (Union) against the Southern states (Confederacy). The Emancipation Proclamation, issued by President Abraham Lincoln in 1863, marked a turning point, signaling a commitment to the abolition of slavery and reshaping the nation's principles.

The Civil War left an indelible mark on the United States, testing its commitment to the principles enshrined in the Constitution. The subsequent Reconstruction era aimed to rebuild the South and address the socio-economic consequences of slavery, but it also marked a period of deep societal upheaval.

Recent American History and Other Important Historical Information

The 20th century unfolded as a period of significant global and domestic challenges, shaping the US into a prominent global power. World Wars I and II saw America emerge as a key player on the world stage, contributing significantly to the Allies' victories.

This century also witnessed pivotal moments in the ongoing struggle for civil rights. For the purpose of eliminating racial discrimination and segregation, the Civil Rights Movement, which was headed by influential individuals such as Martin Luther King Jr., was established. A number of landmark pieces of legislation, such as the Voting Rights Act of 1965 and the Civil Rights Act of 1964, were enacted with the intention of addressing systematic inequities.

As the 20th century progressed, the US navigated through conflicts such as the Korean War, the Vietnam War, and the Gulf War. The Great Depression of the 1930s prompted Franklin D. Roosevelt's New Deal, a series of programs designed to alleviate economic hardships and reshape the role of the federal government in American life.

In the 21st century, the United States faced unprecedented challenges, notably the terrorist attacks on September 11, 2001. This tragic event reshaped US foreign policy, leading to increased national security measures and military interventions in Afghanistan and Iraq.

Additionally, the early 2000s witnessed renewed activism for civil rights, with movements like Black Lives Matter advocating for racial justice and equality. The election of Barack Obama as the first African American president in 2008 marked a historic milestone, reflecting both progress and ongoing challenges in the pursuit of a more inclusive society.

Integrated Civics

Geography

The United States, ranking as the third-largest country globally, boasts a diverse and expansive geographical landscape that plays a pivotal role in shaping the nation's identity. Understanding the geographical features of the United States is essential for those preparing for the USCIS Test.

Overview

The United States is situated between the Atlantic Ocean to the East and the Pacific Ocean to the West, making it a transcontinental country. It shares borders with Canada to the North and Mexico to the South. This strategic location has profoundly influenced the nation's history, economy, and cultural development.

Extensive Coastlines

With coastlines stretching along both the Atlantic and Pacific Oceans, the United States enjoys access to vital maritime routes and a wealth of natural resources. The Atlantic coastline, to the East, features bustling cities and historical sites, while the Pacific coastline, to the West, is characterized by stunning landscapes and vibrant urban centers.

Major Rivers

The United States is home to some of the longest rivers globally, contributing to the nation's economic development and ecological diversity. Notable rivers include the Missouri River, coursing through the heartland, and the iconic Mississippi River, which has played an important role in American history and commerce.

Varied Topography and Climate

The vastness of the United States results in a diverse topography and climate. From the Appalachian Mountains in the East to the Rocky Mountains in the West, the landscape encompasses plains, plateaus, deserts, and forests. This diversity not only influences regional cultures but also supports a range of ecosystems and industries.

Capital and Significant Landmarks

While each state in the US has its capital, the federal capital is Washington, D.C. This iconic city is the seat of the federal government and houses key institutions, including the White House, the Capitol, and the Supreme Court. Washington, D.C., stands as a symbol of democratic governance and national unity.

One of the most iconic symbols of friendship and liberty is the Statue of Liberty, a gift from the people of France in 1886. This copper statue, located on Liberty Island in New York City's Hudson River, represents the enduring values of freedom and democracy. The Statue of Liberty has become an emblematic fixture, welcoming immigrants and symbolizing the nation's commitment to liberty.

US Territories

Beyond the continental United States, there are US territories situated in the Pacific Ocean and the Caribbean Sea. These territories, while not part of the American continent, fall under the jurisdiction of the US government. The territories include Puerto Rico, the US Virgin Islands, American Samoa, the Northern Mariana Islands, and Guam. Each territory has its unique cultural identity and plays an important role in the geopolitical landscape of the US.

- *Puerto Rico:* A vibrant island in the Caribbean with a rich cultural heritage and a unique blend of Spanish, African, and indigenous influences.

- *US Virgin Islands:* Comprising St. Thomas, St. John, and St. Croix, these islands offer stunning landscapes and a diverse cultural tapestry.

- *American Samoa:* Located in the Pacific, American Samoa is known for its lush greenery, coral reefs, and Polynesian cultural traditions.

- *Northern Mariana Islands:* Situated in the western Pacific, this territory boasts a tropical climate and a unique blend of Chamorro and Carolinian cultures.

- *Guam:* Positioned in the western Pacific Ocean, Guam is a strategically important territory with a distinct Chamorro cultural heritage.

Symbols

Symbols hold immense significance in conveying the values, history, and aspirations of a nation. In the US, a myriad of symbols encapsulates the spirit of American identity.

1. The American Flag:

- The Stars and Stripes, with its 13 stripes representing the original colonies and 50 stars for the states, is a powerful symbol of unity and resilience.

- The Pledge of Allegiance is a daily affirmation of loyalty to the flag and the ideals it represents.

2. The Bald Eagle:

- As the national bird and symbol of freedom, the bald eagle embodies strength, majesty, and the enduring spirit of the US.

3. The Statue of Liberty:

- A gift from France, the Statue of Liberty in New York Harbor is a universal symbol of freedom and democracy. Its torch represents enlightenment.

4. The Great Seal:

- The Great Seal of the US features the bald eagle, an olive branch, and arrows, symbolizing peace and readiness for war. The motto "E Pluribus Unum" emphasizes unity.

5. The Liberty Bell:

- Housed in Philadelphia, Pennsylvania, the Liberty Bell has inscriptions that symbolize the struggle for freedom and equality.

6. The White House:

- The official residence and workplace of the President, the White House in Washington, D.C., stands as a symbol of the US government's executive branch.

7. The National Anthem - "The Star-Spangled Banner":

- Written by Francis Scott Key during the War of 1812, the anthem reflects the resilience of American forces in the face of adversity.

8. The Preamble to the US Constitution:

- Beginning with "We the People," the preamble encapsulates the core principles of the Constitution, emphasizing the idea of self-governance.

Holidays

Holidays provide a collective framework for citizens to commemorate historical events, express cultural heritage, and celebrate shared values. The calendar in the US is marked by a wide variety of holidays that showcase the nation's rich history and cultural diversity.

1. **Independence Day - July 4th:**

   - Commemorates the adoption of the Declaration of Independence in 1776.

   - Celebrated with fireworks, parades, barbecues, and patriotic displays.

2. **Thanksgiving:**

   - Originating from the Pilgrims' feast in 1621, Thanksgiving is a time for expressing gratitude for blessings and sharing a meal with loved ones.

3. **Martin Luther King Jr. Day:**

   - Honors the civil rights leader's contributions to racial equality and justice.

4. **Memorial Day:**

   - Honors military personnel who have died in service to their country.

   - Traditionally marked by ceremonies, parades, and visits to cemeteries.

5. **Labor Day:**

   - Recognizes the contributions of American workers and the labor movement.

   - Often considered the unofficial end of summer, celebrated with barbecues and outdoor activities.

6. **Veterans Day:**

   - Honors military veterans who have served in the US Armed Forces.

7. **Presidents' Day:**

   - Originally established to honor George Washington's birthday, it now commemorates all US presidents.

8. **Columbus Day:**

   - Commemorates Christopher Columbus's arrival in the Americas.

- Subject to debates and discussions regarding its historical significance.

9. Christmas:

- A Christian holiday celebrated on December 25th, commemorating the birth of Jesus Christ.

- Marked by gift-giving, decorations, and festive gatherings.

10. New Year's Day:

- Marks the beginning of the new year with celebrations and resolutions.

11. Flag Day - June 14th:

- Commemorates the adoption of the US flag in 1777.

- Often marked by patriotic displays and events.

CHAPTER

USCIS 100 Questions

4

American Government

Principles of American Democracy

1. What is the supreme law of the land?

- The Constitution

Explanation: The USA's Constitution is the country's supreme law. It is the foundation of all federal authorities and imposes significant limitations on the executive branch that safeguard Americans' fundamental freedoms. It was outlined with the cooperation of the state legislative and the sovereign authority of the people.

2. What does the Constitution do?

- Sets up the government
- Defines the government
- Protects basic rights of Americans

Explanation: The Constitution lays out the three primary departments of the federal government as well as the responsibilities that are assigned to each of them. Additionally, it details the essential legislation that the federal government of the US has enacted.

3. The idea of self-government is in the first three words of the Constitution. What are these words?

- We the People

Explanation: The first 3 words of the Constitution "we the people" introduce the concept of self-government. In this context, "we the people" means that it is the citizens themselves who decide to create a government. The words "we the people" also indicate citizens elect representatives to make laws, and the combination of these two characteristics defines the concept of self-government.

4. What is an amendment?

- A change (to the Constitution)
- An addition (to the Constitution)

Explanation: An amendment can be defined as a change or addition to the Constitution.

5. What do we call the first ten amendments to the Constitution?

- The Bill of Rights

Explanation: The first ten (10) Amendments to the Constitution are known as the Bill of Rights. They describe the rights Americans have with regard to their government. They safeguard the individual's civil rights and liberties, such as freedom of speech, press, assembly, and religion.

6. What is one right or freedom from the First Amendment? *

- Speech
- Religion
- Assembly
- Press
- Petition the government

Explanation: The first amendment to the US Constitution protects freedom of speech, assembly, press, religion, and petition to the government.

7. How many amendments does the Constitution have?

- Twenty-seven (27)

Explanation: With time, the American Constitution has adopted changes (amendments) to improve the protection of the rights of its citizens. To date, there have been 27 amendments to the Constitution.

8. What did the Declaration of Independence do?

- Announced our independence (from Great Britain)
- Declared our independence (from Great Britain)
- Said that the US is free (from Great Britain)

Explanation: The thirteen former colonies of the US declared independence from the British Empire through the Declaration of Independence on July 4, 1776. The Declaration of Independence announced the US's independence from the British Empire and declared the country free.

9. What are two rights in the Declaration of Independence?

- Life
- Liberty
- Pursuit of happiness

Explanation: "The truths that we hold to be apparent are that all men are created equal, that they are provided by their Creator with particular inalienable rights, and that among these rights are the right to life, liberty, and the pursuit of happiness." – from the Declaration of Independence

10. What is freedom of religion?

- You can practice any religion, or not practice a religion

Explanation: Religious freedom is the right to follow or not follow any religion. It is a provision of the First Amendment to the US Constitution and applies to anyone who lives in the US.

11. What is the economic system in the US? *

- Capitalist economy
- Market economy

Explanation: The economic system of the US is a mix of capitalist economy and market economy. In the US economy, both privately owned enterprises and the government play important roles.

12. What is the "Rule of Law"?

- Everyone must follow the law
- Leaders must obey the law
- Government must obey the law
- No one is above the law

Explanation: The "Rule of Law" is the concept that expresses how everyone must be subject to the same laws (including governments, legislators, and leaders), that everyone is equal in front of the law, and no one is above the law.

System of Government

13. Name one branch or part of the government. *

- Congress
- Legislative
- President

- Executive
- The courts
- Judicial

Explanation: There are three distinct branches that make up the United States government: the legislative, the executive, and the judicial branches. When it comes to enforcing court decisions, judges are dependent on the executive part of the government.

14. What stops one branch of government from becoming too powerful?

- Checks and balances
- Separation of powers

Explanation: The US government consists of three separate branches: legislative, executive, and judicial. Each of these branches has its own powers that are not proper to the other two. This system was constructed to prevent a single branch of government from having so much power that it could escape the control of the other two branches. This mechanism of having three separate branches, each of which has its own powers and can supervise the other two, is called "Separation of Powers" or "Checks and Balances."

15. Who is in charge of the executive branch?

- The President

Explanation: The executive branch is headed by the President. Vice President and other executive departments and committees are also part of this branch.

16. Who makes federal laws?

- Congress
- Senate and House (of Representatives)
- (US or national) legislature

Explanation: Congress, which comprises the Senate and House of Representatives, has the power to make federal laws. Together, the Senate and the House can also be defined as the legislature.

17. What are the two parts of the US Congress? *

- The Senate (or upper house) and the House (or House of Representatives)

Explanation: Together, the upper house (Senate) and lower house (House of Representatives) form Congress, which forms, in turn, the legislative branch of the US.

18. How many US Senators are there?

- One hundred (100)

Explanation: Each state has 2 senators, while the number of representatives varies from state to state based on the population of each state.

Since there are 50 states in the US and each state elects 2 senators, the Senate consists of a total of one hundred (100) senators.

Senators are elected for a term of 6 years, whereas the representatives are elected for 2 years. Senators are allowed to run for as many terms as they choose. Their responsibility in the Senate is to represent all of the citizens in their state (Similar explanation for questions: 19, 22, 23, and 24).

19. We elect a US Senator for how many years?

- Six (6)

20. Who is one of your state's US Senators now? *

- Responses may differ. If you reside in the District of Columbia or a US territory, indicate that D.C. (or the specific territory) does not have US Senators. To locate your state's US Senators, please visit *senate.gov*.

21. The House of Representatives has how many voting members?

- Four hundred thirty-five (435)

22. We elect a US Representative for how many years?

- Two (2)

23. Name your US Representative.

- Responses may vary. If you reside in a territory with nonvoting Delegates or Resident Commissioners, you may provide the name of that Delegate or Commissioner. Alternatively, stating that the territory has no (voting) Representatives in Congress is acceptable. To find your US Representative, please visit *house.gov*.

24. Who does a US Senator represent?

- All the people in the state where he was elected

25. Why do some states have more Representatives than other states?

- (because of) the state's population
- (because) they have more people
- (because) some states have more people

Explanation: Each state elects a number of representatives that increases as the population increases. The greater the state's population, the more candidates that state can elect.

The US government conducts a census every 10 years to count the citizens of the US. The census determines the total number of people in each state. It also determines how many representatives can be elected within each individual state. Districts are used to partition the state. One representative is elected in each district.

26. We elect a President for how many years?

- Four (4)

Explanation: The twenty-second Amendment, ratified in 1951, restricts Presidents to two four-year terms. No one can serve more than two four-year terms as President.

27. In what month do we vote for President? *

- November

Explanation: Presidential elections are always in November. In 1845, Congress declared November was the ideal month for elections. At the time, the majority of Americans lived on farms. Farmers had finished harvesting their crops by November, which made it easier for them to go out and vote. November was also not as severe as the winter season.

28. What is the name of the President of the US now? *

- Joseph R. Biden
- Joe Biden
- Biden

Explanation: The current President of the US as of today is Joe Biden. However, the President changes after elections. Therefore, you must know the name of the current President at the time you are taking the exam. Visit uscis.gov/citizenship/testupdates for the name of the President of the US.

The updates on the most recent President can be acquired by scanning the following QR code:

29. What is the name of the Vice President of the US now?

- Kamala D. Harris
- Kamala Harris
- Harris

Explanation: The current Vice President of the US as of today is Kamala Harris. However, the Vice President changes after elections; therefore, you must know the name of the current Vice President at the time you are taking the exam. Visit uscis.gov/citizenship/testupdates for the name of the Vice President of the US.

30. If the President can no longer serve, who becomes President?

- The Vice President

Explanation: If the President is unable to serve, the Vice President becomes the President. In the event that both the President and Vice President are unable to serve, the speaker of the House of Representatives becomes the president.

31. If both the President and the Vice President can no longer serve, who becomes President?

- The Speaker of the House

Explanation: Same explanation for question 30

32. Who is the Commander in Chief of the military?

- The President

33. Who signs bills to become laws?

- The President

34. Who vetoes bills?

- The President

35. What does the President's Cabinet do?

- Advises the President

Explanation: The cabinet advises the President on important issues and bills. It consists of the Vice President and the heads of 15 executive departments (which in other legal systems may be called ministries).

36. What are two Cabinet-level positions?

- Secretary of Agriculture
- Secretary of Commerce
- Secretary of Defense
- Secretary of Education
- Secretary of Energy
- Secretary of Health and Human Services
- Secretary of Homeland Security
- Secretary of Housing and Urban Development
- Secretary of the Interior
- Secretary of Labor
- Secretary of State

- Secretary of Transportation
- Secretary of the Treasury
- Secretary of Veterans Affairs
- Attorney General
- Vice President

37. What does the judicial branch do?

- Reviews laws
- Explains laws
- Resolves disputes (disagreements)

Decides if a law goes against the Constitution

38. What is the highest court in the US?

- The Supreme Court

Explanation: The Supreme Court is the country's highest court. The Supreme Court considers if a law violates the Constitution. All other courts must follow the rules laid down by the Supreme Court. The Supreme Court's judgment has to be followed by all states.

39. How many justices are on the Supreme Court?

- Nine (9)

Explanation: The present Supreme Court has nine justices: one Chief Justice and eight Associate Justices. Visit uscis.gov/citizenship/testupdates for the number of justices on the Supreme Court.

40. Who is the Chief Justice of the US now?

- John Roberts
- John G. Roberts, Jr.

Explanation: The current Chief Justice of the US as of today is John G. Roberts. However, the Chief Justice changes. You must know the name of the current Chief Justice at the time you are taking the exam. Visit uscis.gov/citizenship/testupdates for the name of the Chief Justice of the US.

41. Under our Constitution, some powers belong to the federal government. What is one power of the federal government?

- To print money
- To declare war
- To create an army

- To make treaties

42. Under our Constitution, some powers belong to the states. What is one power of the states?

- Provide schooling and education

- Provide protection (police)

- Provide safety (fire departments)

- Give a driver's license

- Approve zoning and land use

43. Who is the Governor of your state now?

- Responses will differ. District of Columbia residents should state that D.C. lacks a Governor. To locate the Governor of your state, please visit *usa.gov/states-and-territories.*

44. What is the capital of your state? *

- There will be a variety of responses. Residents of the District of Columbia should respond by stating that the District of Columbia is not a state and doesn't have a capital. It is the responsibility of the people who live in US territories to identify the capital of their respective territory.

- Below, a complete list of all the capitals of the US

State	Capital
Alabama	Montgomery
Alaska	Juneau
Arizona	Phoenix
Arkansas	Little Rock
California	Sacramento
Colorado	Denver
Connecticut	Hartford
Delaware	Dover
Florida	Tallahassee
Georgia	Atlanta
Hawaii	Honolulu

Idaho	Boise
Illinois	Springfield
Indiana	Indianapolis
Iowa	Des Moines
Kansas	Topeka
Kentucky	Frankfort
Louisiana	Baton Rouge
Maine	Augusta
Maryland	Annapolis
Massachusetts	Boston
Michigan	Lansing
Minnesota	Saint Paul
Mississippi	Jackson
Missouri	Jefferson City
Montana	Helena
Nebraska	Lincoln
Nevada	Carson City
New Hampshire	Concord
New Jersey	Trenton
New Mexico	Santa Fe
New York	Albany
North Carolina	Raleigh
North Dakota	Bismarck
Ohio	Columbus
Oklahoma	Oklahoma City
Oregon	Salem
Pennsylvania	Harrisburg
Rhode Island	Providence
South Carolina	Columbia

South Dakota	Pierre
Tennessee	Nashville
Texas	Austin
Utah	Salt Lake City
Vermont	Montpelier
Virginia	Richmond
Washington	Olympia
West Virginia	Charleston
Wisconsin	Madison
Wyoming	Cheyenne

45. What are the two major political parties in the US? *

- Democratic and Republican

Explanation: The two largest political parties in the US are the Democratic Party and the Republican Party. The Democrats are represented by a donkey symbol. The Republican Party is represented by an elephant symbol.

46. What is the political party of the President now?

- Democratic (party)

Explanation: Visit uscis.gov/citizenship/testupdates for the political party of the President.

47. What is the name of the Speaker of the House of Representatives now?

- Mike Johnson
- Johnson
- James Michael Johnson (birth name)
- (During a grace period ending 1 December, 2023) Patrick McHenry

Visit uscis.gov/citizenship/testupdates for the name of the Speaker of the House of Representatives.

Rights and Responsibilities

48. There are four amendments to the Constitution about who can vote. Describe one of them.

- Citizens eighteen (18) and older (can vote)
- You don't have to pay (a poll tax) to vote
- Any citizen can vote. (Women and men can vote.)
- A male citizen of any race (can vote)

Explanation: Since independence, 4 amendments have been made to the Constitution of the US to ensure the right to vote.

49. What is one responsibility that is only for US citizens? *

- Serve on a jury
- Vote in a federal election

Explanation: Citizens of the US are qualified to vote in federal elections. Voting is essential. However, there is no law forcing citizens to vote. It is solely a moral responsibility. Instead, there is an obligation for citizens to serve on juries when called upon. If a citizen receives a summons to serve on a jury, he or she must comply. A jury is a group of persons who sit in a courtroom to hear a trial. The outcome of the trial is decided by the voting of the jury.

50. Name one right only for US citizens.

- Vote in a federal election
- Run for federal office

Explanation: Only citizens of the US are eligible to vote and apply for state offices. Through their chosen representatives, citizens make laws. There are several legislators and senators in the US who were naturalized citizens. Naturalized citizens, however, are unable to become President.

51. What are two rights of everyone living in the US?

- Freedom of expression
- Freedom of speech
- Freedom of assembly
- Freedom to petition the government
- Freedom of religion
- The right to bear arms

52. What do we show loyalty to when we say the Pledge of Allegiance?

- The US
- The flag

Explanation: As an American citizen, you are expected to pledge allegiance to show loyalty to the flag and the USA. You also pledge to stay loyal to the country, defend and obey the Constitution and the law of the land, and serve the nation when and if needed.

53. What is one promise you make when you become a US citizen?

- Give up loyalty to other countries
- Defend the Constitution and laws of the US
- Obey the laws of the US
- Serve in the US military (if needed)
- Serve (do important work for) the nation (if needed)
- Be loyal to the US

Explanation: To become a US citizen, after passing the exam, you will have to take an oath. During this oath, you will make a series of promises (listed above) that should make explicit your loyalty to the US.

54. How old do citizens have to be to vote for President? *

- Eighteen (18) and older

Explanation: To vote for President, citizens must be 18 years old or older. The Twenty-sixth Amendment was added to the Constitution by Congress and the states in 1971 because the younger generation had broadened its civic and political awareness and so it was considered appropriate to allow them to vote.

55. What are two ways that Americans can participate in their democracy?

- Vote
- Join a political party
- Help with a campaign
- Join a civic group
- Join a community group
- Give an elected official your opinion on an issue
- Call Senators and Representatives
- Publicly support or oppose an issue or policy
- Run for office
- Write to a newspaper

56. When is the last day you can send in federal income tax forms? *

- April 15

Explanation: In the event that you file your tax return for the calendar year and your tax year concludes on December 31st, the deadline to file your federal individual income tax return is typically on April 15th of each year.

57. When must all men register for the Selective Service?

- At age eighteen (18)
- Between eighteen (18) and twenty-six (26)

Explanation: Between the ages of 18 and 26, all men must register for the Selective Service. As you enroll, you are telling the government that you are willing to engage in military service if needed. You are not required to engage in military service unless you wish to do so.

American History

Colonial Period and Independence

58. What is one reason colonists came to America?

- Freedom
- Political liberty
- Religious freedom
- Economic opportunity
- Practice their religion
- Escape persecution

Explanation: The colonists had come to America in search of freedom. Sometimes, they wanted to escape different forms of persecution and have political liberty and be able to practice their religion freely.

59. Who lived in America before the Europeans arrived?

- American Indians
- Native Americans

Explanation: Native Americans (also American Indians) lived in America before the Europeans arrived on this land and colonized it.

60. What group of people was taken to America and sold as slaves?

- Africans
- People from Africa

Explanation: In the early 1500s, millions of people from Africa were brought to America as slaves. Slave masters considered slaves as property for hundreds of years. This was a significant contributing factor to the Civil War. After the Civil War ended in 1865, slavery was abolished. People who had been slaves gained freedom.

61. Why did the colonists fight the British?

- Because of high taxes (taxation without representation)
- Because the British army stayed in their houses (boarding, quartering)
- Because they didn't have self-government

Explanation: The colonists migrated to America in search of freedom. But the British started oppressing them by levying heavy taxes and not allowing them self-government. In addition, British soldiers began to occupy the homes of Americans. This convinced the Americans to fight against the British.

62. Who wrote the Declaration of Independence?

- (Thomas) Jefferson

63. When was the Declaration of Independence adopted?

- July 4, 1776

Explanation to questions 62 & 63: The Declaration of Independence was approved by the colonies on July 4, 1776. The Declaration of Independence was written by Thomas Jefferson. It claimed that the colonies were liberated from British rule. The Declaration was signed by representatives from the 13 colonies. July 4, 1776, therefore, is considered as the date when the USA was officially born as an independent nation.

64. There were 13 original states. Name three.

- New Hampshire
- Massachusetts
- Rhode Island
- Connecticut
- New York
- New Jersey
- Pennsylvania
- Delaware
- Maryland
- Virginia
- North Carolina
- South Carolina

- Georgia

Explanation: New Hampshire, Massachusetts, Rhode Island, Connecticut, New York, New Jersey, Pennsylvania, Delaware, Maryland, Virginia, North Carolina, South Carolina, and Georgia were the first 13 states. The thirteen initial states were the earliest thirteen British territories. To answer this question correctly, you only need to remember the name of 3 out of 13 colonies.

65. What happened at the Constitutional Convention?

- The Constitution was written
- The Founding Fathers wrote the Constitution

Explanation: After the Declaration of Independence, the Constitution was drafted by the "Founding Fathers" during the "Constitutional Convention" in 1787. Fifty-five delegates from 12 of the original 13 states attended the Convention to discuss the system of government and draft the US Constitution. The states decided to approve the Constitution after the Constitutional Convention.

66. When was the Constitution written?

- 1787

67. The Federalist Papers supported the passage of the US Constitution. Name one of the writers.

- (James) Madison
- (Alexander) Hamilton
- (John) Jay
- Publius

Explanation: At the time of the drafting of the Constitution, leaders were divided into two blocs: Federalists and Anti-Federalists. Those who were in favor of the Constitution and who supported it with their "papers," such as James Madison, Alexander Hamilton, and John Jay (the three often wrote under the collective pseudonym "Publius") were the Federalists.

68. What is one thing Benjamin Franklin is famous for?

- US diplomat
- Oldest member of the Constitutional Convention
- First Postmaster General of the US
- Writer of "Poor Richard's Almanac"
- Started the first free libraries

69. Who is the "Father of Our Country"?

- (George) Washington

Explanation: The role George Washington played during the Revolutionary War meant that he was recognized from that time onward as the "Father of Our Country".

70. Who was the first President? *

- (George) Washington

Explanation: George Washington played a leading role in Constitution-making as well as in the American war of independence. He was also the first US President and, for these reasons, he has been honored as the "Father of Our Country".

1800s

71. What territory did the US buy from France in 1803?

- The Louisiana Territory
- Louisiana

Explanation: After gaining independence, the US started to expand its territory and therefore bought The Louisiana Territory, or Louisiana, from France in 1803.

72. Name one war fought by the US in the 1800s.

- War of 1812
- Mexican-American War
- Civil War
- Spanish-American War

Explanation: For more information on this topic, refer to the section "American History"

73. Name the US war between the North and the South.

- The Civil War
- The War between the States

Explanation: It was an internal war between American Northern states (the US, or Union), led by President Abraham Lincoln, and Southern states (the Confederacy). The war was mainly caused by disagreeing positions on slavery, which the northern states wanted to abolish, and on other economic issues.

The war was won by the northern states, which gradually succeeded in forcing the liberation of slaves.

74. Name one problem that led to the Civil War.

- Slavery

- Economic reasons
- States' rights

Explanation: The Civil War started as a result of disputes concerning slavery and other matters, such as economic concerns and states' rights. Some people thought that slavery should be prohibited, while others did not. Enslaved African Americans were used as labor on farms and in cities when the Civil War began in 1861. Many individuals in the South thought that slaves were necessary for their economy and everyday lives. At the same time, people in the North wanted slavery to be abolished. The South fought the Civil War in order to preserve the legality of slavery. In 1865, the North won the war. Slavery was made illegal in every state. (same explanation applies to questions: 75 & 76)

75. What was one important thing that Abraham Lincoln did? *

- Freed the slaves (Emancipation Proclamation)
- Saved (or preserved) the Union
- Led the US during the Civil War

76. What did the Emancipation Proclamation do?

- Freed the slaves
- Freed slaves in the Confederacy
- Freed slaves in the Confederate states
- Freed slaves in most Southern states

77. What did Susan B. Anthony do?

- Fought for women's rights
- Fought for civil rights

Explanation: Susan B. Anthony was a key figure in the women's rights movement and civil rights movement. She delivered talks in favor of women's rights, notably the right to vote. In 1872 Susan B. Anthony even attempted to vote and was arrested. After her death in 1906, the struggle continued, and the Nineteenth Amendment, which granted women the right to vote, was added to the Constitution in 1920.

Recent American History and Other Important Historical Information

78. Name one war fought by the US in the 1900s. *

- World War I
- World War II
- Korean War

- Vietnam War
- (Persian) Gulf War

Explanation: During the 1900s, the US fought in both World Wars 1 & 2, the Cold War, the Korean War, the Vietnam War, and the Gulf War.

79. Who was President during World War I?

- (Woodrow) Wilson

Explanation: Woodrow Wilson was the American President at the time of World War I. He did not join the war until late 1917.

80. Who was President during the Great Depression and World War II?

- (Franklin) Roosevelt

Explanation: Elected in 1933, Franklin D. Roosevelt was the President of the US during the Great Depression and World War II. The term "Great Depression" is used to refer to the period, from 1929 to 1939, during which the US economy fell precipitously, banks went bankrupt, and many people were unemployed. Franklin D. Roosevelt attempted to repair the economy. In 1941, the US entered World War II. Americans fought alongside Great Britain, the Soviet Union, France, and China against Germany, Italy, and Japan. Franklin D. Roosevelt served as President until his death in 1945.

81. Who did the US fight in World War II?

- Japan, Germany, and Italy

Explanation: In World War Two, the US fought against Germany, Italy, and Japan. After Japan bombed Pearl Harbor (Hawaii) in 1941, the US entered World War II. Germany and Italy had Japan as an ally. They joined forces to create the "Axis powers." In 1945, the US and its allies defeated Japan, Germany, and Italy.

82. Before he was President, Eisenhower was a general. What war was he in?

- World War II

Explanation: During World War II, President Dwight D. Eisenhower served as a general, and commanded the American Army and the allied forces in Western Europe. He was a popular military hero when he returned from WWII. In 1953, he was elected President.

83. During the Cold War, what was the main concern of the US?

- Communism

Explanation: After the end of World War II, The US and USSR started a cold war that was an ideological war between communism and capitalism. The US was concerned about the spread of communism to other countries. The US wanted to spread freedom and liberty in the world through democracy and capitalism.

84. What movement tried to end racial discrimination?

- Civil rights (movement)

Explanation: From 1954 through 1968, the civil rights movement was a political ideology and movement in the US to end structural racial segregation, discrimination, and marginalization throughout the country. One of the most important leaders of this movement was Martin Luther King, Jr.

85. What did Martin Luther King, Jr. do? *

- Fought for civil rights
- Worked for equality for all Americans

Explanation: Under the leadership of Martin Luther King, Jr., Americans fought for the freedom and civil rights of African Americans and demanded equal rights for all citizens which were ensured, and African Americans were given voting and other fundamental rights.

86. What major event happened on September 11, 2001, in the US?

- Terrorists attacked the US

Explanation: It was one of the most tragic events in American history. The terrorist attack on the Twin Towers in New York City on September 11th, 2001, took the lives of thousands of innocent American citizens.

87. Name one American Indian tribe in the US.

- Cherokee
- Navajo
- Sioux
- Chippewa
- Choctaw
- Pueblo
- Apache
- Iroquois
- Creek
- Blackfeet
- Seminole
- Cheyenne

- Arawak
- Shawnee
- Mohegan
- Huron
- Oneida
- Lakota
- Crow
- Teton
- Hopi
- Inuit

Integrated Civics

Geography

88. Name one of the two longest rivers in the US.

- Missouri (River)
- Mississippi (River)

Explanation: The Missouri River and the Mississippi River are the two longest rivers in the US. The Missouri River is the longest river in the US. It originates in the Rocky Mountains and runs 2,341 miles, first eastward and then southward before flowing into the Mississippi River. The Mississippi River flows through 10 states in the US. It begins in Minnesota, near the border with Canada. It concludes in Louisiana.

89. What ocean is on the West Coast of the US?

- Pacific (Ocean)

Explanation: The Pacific Ocean bathes the entire west coast of the US.

90. What ocean is on the East Coast of the US?

- Atlantic (Ocean)

Explanation: The US is bordered on the East by the Atlantic Ocean. This ocean extends from the American East coast to Europe and Africa. Another interesting fact is that the initial 13 colonies had been founded along the coast of the Atlantic Ocean.

91. Name one US territory.

- Puerto Rico

- US Virgin Islands
- American Samoa
- Northern Mariana Islands
- Guam

Explanation: The "US territories" are territories located between the Pacific Ocean and the Caribbean Sea that, while not part of the American continent, are under the jurisdiction of the US government.

92. Name one state that borders Canada.

- Maine
- New Hampshire
- Vermont
- New York
- Pennsylvania
- Ohio
- Michigan
- Minnesota
- North Dakota
- Montana
- Idaho
- Washington
- Alaska

93. Name one state that borders Mexico.

- California
- Arizona
- New Mexico
- Texas

94. What is the capital of the US? *

- Washington, D.C.

95. Where is the Statue of Liberty? *

- New York (Harbor)
- Liberty Island

[Also acceptable are New Jersey, near New York City, and on the Hudson River.]

Explanation: In 1886, the people of France gave a gift of friendship to the US in the form of a copper statue that is called "The statue of Liberty," installed at Liberty Island on the Hudson River in New York City (harbor).

Symbols

96. Why does the flag have 13 stripes?

- Because there were 13 original colonies
- Because the stripes represent the original colonies

Explanation: Same explanation as question 97

97. Why does the flag have 50 stars? *

- Because there is one star for each state
- Because each star represents a state
- Because there are 50 states

Explanation: The American flag has 13 stripes and 50 stars. The stripes symbolize the former 13 colonies, whereas the stars symbolize the current 50 American states. Each star represents a state, and there is one star for every state. (Same explanation for question: 96)

98. What is the name of the national anthem?

- The Star-Spangled Banner

Explanation: The national anthem is called "The Star-Spangled Banner." The anthem revolves around the American flag. During the War of 1812, British ships stormed Fort McHenry in Baltimore one night. Throughout the night, bombs burst. From a ship, an American named Francis Scott Key saw the battle. He was concerned that the US would lose the fight. The next day, he noticed the American flag flapping in the breeze. He was aware that the US had won the fight. Then he composed "The Star-Spangled Banner," which is currently the US national anthem.

Holidays

99. When do we celebrate Independence Day? *

- July 4

Explanation: The thirteen former colonies of the US declared independence from the British Empire through the Declaration of Independence on July 4, 1776. July 4th has been ever since celebrated as a national holiday each year to commemorate the Independence Day of the country.

100. Name two national US holidays.

- New Year's Day
- Martin Luther King, Jr. Day
- Presidents' Day
- Memorial Day
- Juneteenth
- Independence Day
- Labor Day
- Columbus Day
- Veterans Day
- Thanksgiving
- Christmas

CHAPTER 5

Exclusive Bonuses:
Printable Flashcards and Audiobook

Welcome to our exclusive bonus package designed to bolster your study for the U.S. Citizenship Test! Now, in addition to our detailed flashcards, you'll also gain access to the audiobook of the guidebook. Simply aim your smartphone or tablet's camera at the QR code provided below, and you'll be directed to a folder where you can both access the audiobook and print out the flashcards.

Each flashcard set includes questions on the left and their corresponding answers on the right. After printing, cut out each flashcard along the indicated lines, then paste them back to back so that the question is on one side and the answer is on the other. This format allows for convenient study sessions and efficient memorization of essential citizenship test content.

The addition of the audiobook offers an invaluable tool: listen to it while on the go or during your relaxation time at home. This dual approach, visual and auditory, significantly enhances your chances of memorizing and understanding the material, making your study time more dynamic and less strenuous.

Happy studying and best of luck on your journey to U.S. citizenship!

Tips for Effective Learning with Flashcards:

1. **Break Information into Digestible Chunks:** Use each flashcard to focus on one specific concept, vocabulary word, or civics question. Breaking information into smaller, digestible chunks makes it easier to process and remember.

2. **Utilize Active Recall:** When reviewing flashcards, cover the answer or question and try to recall it from memory before checking. This active recall technique strengthens your memory and reinforces learning.

3. **Create Mnemonics or Memory Aids:** For complex concepts or information, create mnemonic devices or memory aids to help you remember. Associating information with vivid imagery or acronyms can make it easier to recall during the test.

4. **Mix Up the Order:** Shuffle the flashcards or mix up the order when reviewing to prevent rote memorization. Randomizing the order challenges your brain to retrieve information more effectively.

5. **Track Your Progress:** While you are going over the flashcards, make sure to keep track of your progress. Take note of the areas in which you excel and those in which you may need some work, and alter your approach to studying appropriately.

6. **Review Regularly:** Consistency is key to effective learning with flashcards. Set aside dedicated study sessions and commit to regular review to reinforce your understanding and retention of the material.

With these downloadable flashcards and tips for effective learning, you have a valuable resource to support your study efforts and help you prepare for the US citizenship test. Incorporate them into your study routine, stay focused, and believe in your ability to succeed. Good luck on your journey to becoming a proud US citizen!

CHAPTER

6

Practical English Test Preparation

Speaking Test Practice

Practice Test 1

In this speaking test, we will simulate interview scenarios that mimic the format and vocabulary used in USCIS (US Citizenship and Immigration Services) interviews. These scenarios will cover a range of conversational topics relevant to the naturalization process, allowing applicants to practice their speaking skills and demonstrate their understanding of key concepts. Let's begin:

Scenario 1: Introduction and Personal Background

Interviewer: Good morning. Please have a seat. Can you please state your full name for the record?

Applicant: Good morning. My name is [Applicant's Full Name].

Interviewer: Thank you. Can you confirm your current address?

Applicant: Yes, I currently reside at [Applicant's Address].

Interviewer: Great. Now, could you tell me where you were born and your date of birth?

Applicant: I was born in [Country of Birth] on [Date of Birth].

Interviewer: Thank you. How long have you been living in the US?

Applicant: I have been living in the US for [Number of Years].

Interviewer: Excellent. And what is your marital status?

Applicant: I am [Marital Status].

Interviewer: Thank you for providing that information. Now, let's move on to the next topic.

Scenario 2: Residence and Physical Presence Requirements

Interviewer: Can you confirm that you have maintained continuous residence in the US since obtaining your green card?

Applicant: Yes, I have continuously resided in the US since becoming a permanent resident.

Interviewer: Have you traveled outside of the US for any extended periods during that time?

Applicant: Yes, I have traveled outside the US, but always for short trips and never for an extended period.

Interviewer: Can you provide details about your recent travels outside the US?

Applicant: Of course. I traveled to [Destination] for [Purpose of Travel] from [Dates of Travel].

Interviewer: Thank you for providing that information. Let's proceed to the next topic.

Scenario 3: US Government and History

Interviewer: Can you tell me about one of the founding documents of the US?

Applicant: One of the founding documents of the US is the Declaration of Independence, which was adopted on July 4, 1776.

Interviewer: Thank you. Now, can you name one of the original 13 colonies?

Applicant: Yes, one of the original 13 colonies is Massachusetts.

Interviewer: Great. Now, let's move on to the final topic.

Scenario 4: Rights and Responsibilities of US Citizens

Interviewer: Can you name one right guaranteed by the First Amendment to the US Constitution?

Applicant: Yes, one right guaranteed by the First Amendment is freedom of speech.

Interviewer: Thank you. Now, can you tell me about one responsibility that US citizens have?

Applicant: One responsibility of US citizens is to serve on a jury when called upon.

Interviewer: Excellent. You have demonstrated a good understanding of the rights and responsibilities of US citizens. That concludes our interview. Thank you for your time.

Applicant: Thank you for the opportunity.

Practice Test 2

Scenario 1: English Language Proficiency

Interviewer: I'd like to test your English language proficiency. Can you tell me about your daily routine?

Applicant: Sure. In the mornings, I usually wake up, have breakfast, and then head to work. I work as [Occupation]. After work, I spend time with my family and sometimes go for a walk in the evening.

Interviewer: Thank you. Can you describe your favorite holiday or celebration in the US?

Applicant: My favorite holiday in the US is Independence Day, also known as the Fourth of July. It's a time when Americans come together to celebrate their freedom and heritage.

Interviewer: Excellent. Your English proficiency seems very good. Let's move on to the next topic.

Scenario 2: US Government and History

Interviewer: Can you name one of the founding fathers of the US?

Applicant: Yes, one of the founding fathers is Thomas Jefferson.

Interviewer: Thank you. Now, can you name one of the original 13 colonies?

Applicant: Yes, one of the original 13 colonies is Pennsylvania.

Interviewer: Correct. Let's proceed to the final topic.

Scenario 3: Rights and Responsibilities of US Citizens

Interviewer: Can you name one right guaranteed by the Constitution's Bill of Rights?

Applicant: Yes, one right guaranteed by the Bill of Rights is the freedom of religion.

Interviewer: Thank you. Now, can you tell me about a responsibility that US citizens have?

Applicant: One responsibility of US citizens is to participate in the democratic process by voting in elections.

Interviewer: Excellent. You have demonstrated a good understanding of citizenship concepts. That concludes our interview. Thank you for your time.

Applicant: Thank you for the opportunity to interview.

Scenario 4: Civic Engagement

Interviewer: Can you explain the significance of voting in a democracy?

Applicant: Voting is a fundamental right and responsibility in a democracy. It allows citizens to participate in the decision-making process and shape the direction of their country. By voting, individuals can voice their opinions and contribute to the selection of leaders who represent their interests.

Interviewer: Thank you. Now, can you describe any experience you've had volunteering in your community?

Applicant: Certainly. I have volunteered at a local food bank, helping to distribute meals to those in need. It was a rewarding experience to give back to my community and support individuals facing food insecurity.

Interviewer: That's commendable. Let's move on to the next scenario.

Scenario 5: Cultural Integration

Interviewer: Can you share how you have embraced American culture since moving here?

Applicant: Since moving to the US, I have embraced American traditions such as celebrating Thanksgiving and Independence Day with my family and friends. I have also enjoyed exploring American cuisine and learning about the diverse cultural heritage of this country.

Interviewer: Thank you. Now, can you describe a cultural event or festival in your hometown?

Applicant: In my hometown, we celebrate [insert festival or event], which is a vibrant celebration of our cultural heritage. It involves traditional music, dance, and cuisine, and brings the community together in joyous festivities.

Interviewer: That sounds wonderful. That concludes our interview. Thank you for your time.

Applicant: Thank you for the opportunity to discuss these important topics.

Practice Test 3

This section comprises a set of questions replicating those you will be asked during the first part of the Interview, the one where the USCIS officer will ask you questions that, in most cases, relate to topics similar to those addressed by filling out the naturalization application.

By identifying the correct answers in this section, it will become easier for you to answer the questions during the real Interview.

1. Mr. John Fitzgerald Kennedy was the 35th President of the US.

a) What is Mr. John Fitzgerald Kennedy's first name?

b) What is Mr. John Fitzgerald Kennedy's family/last name?

c) What is Mr. John Fitzgerald Kennedy's middle name?

2. Alex was born in Canada but now lives in Texarkana, Texas. Her address is 688 Hall Place, Apt. C6, Texarkana, Texas 03866.

a) What is Alex's country of birth?

b) Where does Alex currently live?

c) What is Alex's street name?

d) What is Alex's apartment number?

e) What is Alex's zip code?

3. Bill is a carpenter at Custom Hardwood Doors. He has been working there for 3 years.

a) What is the name of Bill's Employer?

b) What is Bill's occupation?

4. Bob has two daughters and a son. His wife divorced him last month.

a) How many children does Bob have?

b) What is Bob's marital status?

5. Marisa is living in Chicago, Illinois. Previously, she lived in Philadelphia, Pennsylvania.

a) Where does Marisa live now?

b) Where did Marisa live before that?

6. Every year, Jeff takes three trips. He goes to Bali, Indonesia, for recreation every summer for a month. He visits his parents in Florida during Christmas for 10 days. He also visits his friends in Italy for a week.

a) How much time does Jeff spend outside the US every year?

b) How many trips does he take outside the US?

c) Which two countries does Jeff visit each year?

d) Where does he go in summer?

e) How many trips does he take inside the US?

f) Which US states does Jeff visit each year?

Practice Test 1 - Answers

Question 1

a) John

b) Kennedy

c) Fitzgerald

Question 2

a) Canada

b) Texas

c) Hall place

d) C6

e) 03866

Question 3

a) Custom Hardwood Doors

b) Carpenter

Question 4

a) 3

b) Divorced

Question 5

a) Chicago

b) Pennsylvania

Question 6

a) 5 weeks

b) 2 trips

c) Italy and Indonesia

d) Bali, Indonesia

e) One

f) Florida

Reading Test Practice

The following are practice sentences for reading. They contain all the words that you must know how to read. Read the sentences. Have a friend or relative listen to see if you are reading the sentences correctly. As with everything else, the more you practice, the better you will do.

Practice Test 1

1. Pay here.

2. We want to pay.

3. We want to vote.

4. What is Flag Day?

5. Why be the first?

6. When is Labor Day?

7. Be first to vote.

8. Where is the south?

9. Where do we pay?

10. The senators are here.

11. When do people vote?

12. Where is the north?

13. Who elects Congress?

14. When is Memorial Day?

15. When does one vote?

16. What is Thanksgiving?

17. What is the Congress?

18. We lived in the south.

19. When does Flag Day come?

20. Who can be a citizen?

21. Why do people vote?

22. America is in the north.

23. The capital is a city.

24. When is Independence Day?

25. America is a country.

26. When is Presidents' Day?

27. Where is the largest city?

28. The President was here.

29. When do the people vote?

30. We can meet the President.

Practice Test 2

1. Most senators are here.

2. We can meet the Senators.

3. We want to do what is right.

4. The largest city is here.

5. Who was Abraham Lincoln?

6. The White House is here.

7. Come here on Labor Day.

8. Where is the dollar bill?

9. Who elects the US senators?

10. How does a citizen vote?

11. Where is the White House?

12. When is Independence Day?

13. The capital is in the north.

14. Name a state in the south.

15. Abraham Lincoln lived here.

16. The south has many people.

17. People lived in many states.

18. Who was George Washington?

19. Who is the first citizen?

20. A citizen has to vote here.

21. Was Abraham Lincoln a President?

22. Where do we meet the senators?

23. What is the Bill of Rights?

24. Name one right of a citizen.

25. Who lives in the White House?

26. People come in many colors.

27. What is the largest state?

28. Why do people want to vote?

29. Most states are in the north.

30. What is the largest country?

Practice Test 3

1. Senators meet in the capital.

2. The north has the most people.

3. The American flag has colors.

4. Who was the second President?

5. The people elect the Congress.

6. Abraham Lincoln was a President.

7. George Washington lived here.

8. Many states are in the south.

9. The US is a country.

10. What is the Bill of Rights?

11. Many people lived in the south.

12. The government has many senators.

13. What country is south of the US?

14. Who is the Father of Our Country?

15. Senators meet in the capital city.

16. The largest state is in the north.

17. The second name is Abraham Lincoln.

18. The government is for the people.

19. How many rights do citizens have?

20. What country is north of the US?

21. How many Senators are in Congress?

22. What is the name of the President?

23. Abraham Lincoln lived in the north.

24. Where is the capital of the country?

25. The President is the first citizen.

26. When are Columbus Day and Thanksgiving?

27. US people have many rights.

28. The President lives in the White House.

29. George Washington is on the dollar bill.

30. George Washington was the first President.

31. Presidents' Day and Memorial Day come first.

32. The second President lived in the south.

33. The capital of the US is a city.

34. How many colors does the American flag have?

35. Citizens vote for the government of America.

36. Why is George Washington on the dollar bill?

37. Abraham Lincoln was a US President.

38. What is the name of the Father of Our Country?

39. The father of our country is George Washington.

40. Where is the largest city in the US?

Writing Test Practice 3 test

Below, is a list of sentences of the same type as those you will be asked to write during the writing exam and constructed with the same terms shown in the official USCIS Writing Vocabulary List.

Practice by asking someone next to you to read each sentence to you and try writing it. When you have finished writing, go back and look at sentences from the examples to check that you have written them correctly.

Practice Test 1

1. We pay taxes.

2. The flag is here.

3. Citizens can vote.

4. People can be free.

5. Alaska is a state.

6. Pay for the flag.

7. We want to vote.

8. Citizens pay taxes.

9. We lived in Canada.

10. Pay here for the flag.

11. Most people can vote.

12. Flag Day is in June.

13. Pay for the largest flag.

14. The largest flag is free.

15. Senators vote for taxes.

16. One state is Delaware.

17. People want to be free.

18. Adams was President

19. Washington is one State.

20. The Senators vote here.

21. Citizens elect the Senators.

22. Alaska is the largest state.

23. Alaska is north of Mexico.

24. Mexico is south of Canada.

25. Memorial Day is in May.

26. Independence Day is in July.

27. Labor Day is in September.

28. Columbus Day is in October.

29. The Senators want to vote.

30. The White House is white.

31. Delaware is north of Mexico.

32. Citizens vote in November.

33. Come to the White House.

34. Is Canada the largest state?

35. American Indians can vote.

36. One Right is the right to vote.

37. The largest state is Alaska.

38. Thanksgiving is in November.

39. Citizens elect the President.

40. We the citizens elect Congress.

Practice Test 2

1. The White House is here.

2. American Indians in Alaska vote.

3. The second President was Adams.

4. The right to vote is one right.

5. Citizens want freedom of speech.

6. The President meets the people.

7. The White House is in the capital.

8. US citizens pay taxes.

9. Is Washington, D.C. in Washington?

10. Congress meets in Washington, D.C.

11. California has the most people.

12. Presidents day is in February.

13. Washington is on the dollar bill.

14. Unites States citizens can vote.

15. Lincoln lived in the White House.

16. The flag is red, white and blue.

17. American Indians lived in Alaska.

18. Freedom of speech is one Right.

19. California is south of Washington.

20. The President lives in Washington, D.C.

21. New York City has the most people.

22. Adams was the second President.

23. One Right is freedom of speech.

24. Freedom of speech is one Right.

25. Washington was the first President.

26. The first President was Washington.

27. The people lived in Washington.

28. People come during Thanksgiving.

29. We can come to the White House.

30. Canada is north of the US.

31. Mexico is south of the US.

32. Delaware is south of New York City.

33. New York City is in the US.

34. Come during Independence Day.

35. Most people have one dollar bill.

36. New York City is the largest one.

37. New York City is north of Delaware.

38. The White House is in Washington, D.C.

39. The US has fifty (50) states.

40. The President lives in the White House.

Practice Test 3

1. Washington is the Father of Our Country.

2. People come here for freedom of speech.

3. Congress has one hundred (100) Senators.

4. The White House has the largest flag.

5. We have the Right of freedom of speech.

6. The Father of Our Country is Washington.

7. Lincoln was President during the Civil War.

8. Alaska is the largest of the 50 (fifty) states.

9. People come to the US to be free.

10. People want American Indians to vote.

11. The President meets people at the White House.

12. Citizens elect the President and the Senators.

13. The President and the Senators pay taxes.

14. During the Civil War the President was Lincoln.

15. American Indians lived first in the US.

16. The capital of the US is Washington, D.C.

17. American Indians lived in the US first.

18. One President lived in Washington D.C. and New York City.

19. Presidents' Day and Memorial Day come before Thanksgiving.

20. The one hundred (100) Senators vote in Washington, D.C.

21. Americans celebrate Columbus Day every year.

22. My grandmother meets us on Thanksgiving.

23. Every American citizen must pay his taxes.

24. I will visit Mexico during the holidays.

25. A red flag is a sign of danger.

26. My sister lives in California.

27. Labor Day is celebrated on the first Monday in September.

28. Abraham Lincoln was the 16th President of the US.

29. American citizens are free to follow any religion.

30. There are 100 senators in the upper house of Congress.

CHAPTER

Civics Practice Tests

7

In this section, you'll encounter 10 sets of questions randomly selected from a pool of 100 official USCIS questions. Each set will contain 10 questions, as 10 is the maximum number of questions you could be asked during the civics test. It's important to note that in the actual test, these questions will be asked orally, and you'll need to respond orally as well. Furthermore, you only need to answer 6 questions correctly to pass this portion of the naturalization exam.

Civics Practice Test 1

Questions:

1. Which of the laws is considered to be the highest?

2. What are the functions of the Constitution?

3. What number of senators and representatives are there in the House of Representatives?

4. How many years do we choose to serve as a representative for the United States?

5. Name your representative in the United States.

6. The Constitution has four amendments that address the question of who is eligible to vote. Explain one of them in detail.

7. What was it that Martin Luther King Jr. accomplished?

8. What major event happened on September 11, 2001, in the United States?

9. Name one of the American Indian tribes that are located in the US.

10. What is the name of one of the two rivers that are the longest in the US.

Answers:

Question 1

- The Constitution

Question 2

- Sets up the government
- Defines the government
- Protects basic rights of Americans

Question 3

- Four hundred thirty-five (435)

Question 4

- Two (2)

Question 5

- Responses may vary. If you reside in a territory with nonvoting Delegates or Resident Commissioners, you may provide the name of that Delegate or Commissioner. Alternatively, stating that the territory has no (voting) Representatives in Congress is acceptable. To find your US Representative, please visit house.gov.

Question 6

- Citizens eighteen (18) and older (can vote)
- You don't have to pay (a poll tax) to vote
- Any citizen can vote. (Women and men can vote.)
- A male citizen of any race (can vote)

Question 7

- Fought for civil rights
- Worked for equality for all Americans

Question 8

- Terrorists attacked the US

Question 9

- Cherokee
- Navajo

- Sioux
- Chippewa
- Choctaw
- Pueblo
- Apache
- Iroquois
- Creek
- Blackfeet
- Seminole
- Cheyenne
- Arawak
- Shawnee
- Mohegan
- Huron
- Oneida
- Lakota
- Crow
- Teton
- Hopi
- Inuit

Question 10

- Missouri (River)
- Mississippi (River)

Civics Practice Test 2

Questions:

1. The Constitution introduces the concept of self-government in the very first three words of the document. Where can I find these words? An amendment is what exactly?

2. Who does a senator in the United States represent?

3. What are the reasons that certain states have a greater number of Representatives than others?

4. For what number of years do we choose to elect a President?

5. Which of the following is a responsibility that is exclusive to citizens of the US?

6. Eisenhower served as a general prior to his election to the presidency. To what conflict was he a party?

7. What was the primary worry of the USA throughout the time of the Cold War?

8. What social movement made an effort to put an end to racial discrimination?

9. In the US, which ocean is located on the west coast of the country?

Answers:

Question 1

- We the People

Question 2

- A change (to the Constitution)
- An addition (to the Constitution)

Question 3

- All the people in the state where he was elected

Question 4

- (because of) the state's population
- (because) they have more people
- (because) some states have more people

Question 5

- Four (4)

Question 6

- Serve on a jury
- Vote in a federal election

Question 7

- World War II

Question 8

- Communism

Question 9

- Civil rights (movement)

Question 10

- Pacific (Ocean)

Civics Practice Test 3

Questions:

1. What is the name given to the first ten amendments that were added to the Constitution?

2. What is an example of a right or freedom that is guaranteed under the First Amendment?*

3. When is the month that we cast our votes for the President?*

4. I would like to know the name of the current President of the US of America.*

5. Who is the current Vice President of the USA, and what is their name?

6. Name one right that is exclusive to citizens of the US.

7. On the occasion of World War I, who served as President?

8. During the Great Depression and World War II, who was the President of the United States?

9. During World War II, the USA fought against whom?

10. In the US, which ocean is located on the east coast of the country?

Answers:

Question 1

- The Bill of Rights

Question 2

- Speech
- Religion
- Assembly
- Press
- Petition the government

Question 3

- November

Question 4

- Joseph R. Biden
- Joe Biden
- Biden

Question 5

- Kamala D. Harris
- Kamala Harris
- Harris

Question 6

- Vote in a federal election
- Run for federal office

Question 7

- (Woodrow) Wilson

Question 8

- (Franklin) Roosevelt

Question 9

- Japan, Germany, and Italy

Question 10

- Atlantic (Ocean)

Civics Practice Test 4

Questions:

1. The Constitution has been amended over the course of how many years?

2. What was the purpose of the Declaration of Independence?

3. Who will succeed the President in the event that he or she is unable to continue serving?

4. Who will take over as President in the event that both the President and the Vice President are unable to continue serving?

5. Who holds the position of Commander in Chief of the US Armed Forces?

6. What are two rights that are guaranteed to every person who resides in the US?

7. What was the effect of the Emancipation Proclamation?

8. How did Susan B. Anthony accomplish her goals?

9. Please name one conflict that the USA fought throughout the 1900s.

10. Name a territory that is part of the US.

Answers:

Question 1

- Twenty-seven (27)

Question 2

- Announced our independence (from Great Britain)
- Declared our independence (from Great Britain)
- Said that the US is free (from Great Britain)

Question 3

- The Vice President

Question 4

- The Speaker of the House

Question 5

- The President

Question 6

- Freedom of expression
- Freedom of speech
- Freedom of assembly
- Freedom to petition the government
- Freedom of religion
- The right to bear arms

Question 7

- Freed the slaves

- Freed slaves in the Confederacy
- Freed slaves in the Confederate states
- Freed slaves in most Southern states

Question 8

- Fought for women's rights
- Fought for civil rights

Question 9

- World War I
- World War II
- Korean War
- Vietnam War
- (Persian) Gulf War

Question 10

- Puerto Rico
- US Virgin Islands
- American Samoa
- Northern Mariana Islands
- Guam

Civics Practice Test 5

Questions:

1. The Declaration of Independence outlines two rights that citizens are entitled to.

2. What exactly is meant by the term "religious freedom"?

3. Who is responsible for signing bills into law?

4. Who has the power to veto bills?

5. What are the obligations of the President's Cabinet?

6. When we recite the Pledge of Allegiance, is it to what do we demonstrate our allegiance?

7. Name the conflict that took place in the US between the North and the South.

8. Please name one of the issues that contributed to the outbreak of the Civil War.

9. Which of Abraham Lincoln's actions was considered to be the most significant?*

10. Can you name one state that shares a border with Canada?

Answers:

Question 1

- Life
- Liberty
- Pursuit of happiness

Question 2

- You can practice any religion, or not practice a religion

Question 3

- The President

Question 4

- The President

Question 5

- Advises the President

Question 6

- The US
- The flag

Question 7

- The Civil War
- The War between the States

Question 8

- Slavery
- Economic reasons
- States' rights

Question 9

- Freed the slaves (Emancipation Proclamation)
- Saved (or preserved) the Union

- Led the US during the Civil War

Question 10

- Maine
- New Hampshire
- Vermont
- New York
- Pennsylvania
- Ohio
- Michigan
- Minnesota
- North Dakota
- Montana
- Idaho
- Washington
- Alaska

Civics Practice Test 6

Questions:

1. What kind of economic system does the USA have?*

2. Why is it called the "rule of law"?

3. Where can I find two posts at the Cabinet level?

4. When you acquire a citizenship of the US, what is one pledge that you make to yourself?

5. What are the functions of the judicial branch?

6. The US Supreme Court is the highest court in the country.

7. Where did the first President come from?*

8. The USA purchased a certain land from France in the year 1803.

9. There was one war that the USA fought in the 1800s.

10. Which state is the only one that borders Mexico?

Answers:

Question 1

- Capitalist economy
- Market economy

Question 2

- Everyone must follow the law
- Leaders must obey the law
- Government must obey the law
- No one is above the law

Question 3

- Secretary of Agriculture
- Secretary of Commerce
- Secretary of Defense
- Secretary of Education
- Secretary of Energy
- Secretary of Health and Human Services
- Secretary of Homeland Security
- Secretary of Housing and Urban Development
- Secretary of the Interior
- Secretary of Labor
- Secretary of State
- Secretary of Transportation
- Secretary of the Treasury
- Secretary of Veterans Affairs
- Attorney General
- Vice President

Question 4

- Give up loyalty to other countries
- Defend the Constitution and laws of the US
- Obey the laws of the US

- Serve in the US military (if needed)
- Serve (do important work for) the nation (if needed)
- Be loyal to the US

Question 5

- Reviews laws
- Explains laws
- Resolves disputes (disagreements)
- Decides if a law goes against the Constitution

Question 6

- The Supreme Court

Question 7

- (George) Washington

Question 8

- The Louisiana Territory
- Louisiana

Question 9

- War of 1812
- Mexican-American War
- Civil War
- Spanish-American War

Question 10

- California
- Arizona
- New Mexico
- Texas

Civics Practice Test 7

Questions:

1. What type of economic system does the USA have?*
2. What is the reason behind the term "rule of law"?

3. In what location may I locate two positions at the Cabinet level?

4. In the process of obtaining citizenship in the US, what is one promise that you make to yourself personally?

5. Which functions does the judicial branch of government perform?

6. The highest court in the US is the Supreme Court of the US.

7. From what background did the first President originate?*

8. In the year 1803, the USA made a purchase from France of a particular piece of land.

9. During the 1800s, the USA participated in one conflict.

10. One of the states is the only one that shares a border with Mexico.

Answers:

Question 1

- Congress
- Legislative
- President
- Executive
- The courts
- Judicial

Question 2

- Checks and balances
- Separation of powers

Question 3

- Nine (9)

Question 4

- John Roberts
- John G. Roberts, Jr.

Question 5

- To print money
- To declare war
- To create an army

- To make treaties

Question 6

- Eighteen (18) and older

Question 7

- (James) Madison
- (Alexander) Hamilton
- (John) Jay
- Publius

Question 8

- US diplomat
- Oldest member of the Constitutional Convention
- First Postmaster General of the US
- Writer of "Poor Richard's Almanac"
- Started the first free libraries

Question 9

- (George) Washington

Question 10

- Washington, D.C.

Civics Practice Test 8

Questions:

1. Who occupies the position of head of the executive branch?

2. Who is responsible for drafting federal laws?

3. According to our Constitution, certain powers are to be delegated to the states.

4. What is one of the powers that the states possess?

5. Who is now serving as the Governor of your state?

6. What is the name of the state capital in your state?

7. What are two ways that citizens of the US can participate in their democratic process?

8. In the beginning, there were thirteen states. Call out three.

9. At the Constitutional Convention, what were the events that took place?

10. Do you know when the Constitution was written?

11. What is the location of the Statue of Liberty?

Answers:

Question 1

- The President

Question 2

- Congress
- Senate and House (of Representatives)
- (US or national) legislature

Question 3

- Provide schooling and education
- Provide protection (police)
- Provide safety (fire departments)
- Give a driver's license
- Approve zoning and land use

Question 4

- Responses will differ. District of Columbia residents should state that D.C. lacks a Governor. To locate the Governor of your state, please visit usa.gov/states-and-territories.

Question 5

- There will be a variety of responses. Residents of the District of Columbia should respond by stating that the District of Columbia is not a state and lacks a capital. It is the responsibility of the people who live in US territories to identify the capital of their respective territories.

Question 6

- Vote
- Join a political party
- Help with a campaign
- Join a civic group

- Join a community group
- Give an elected official your opinion on an issue
- Call Senators and Representatives
- Publicly support or oppose an issue or policy
- Run for office
- Write to a newspaper

Question 7

- New Hampshire
- Massachusetts
- Rhode Island
- Connecticut
- New York
- New Jersey
- Pennsylvania
- Delaware
- Maryland
- Virginia
- North Carolina
- South Carolina
- Georgia

Question 8

- The Constitution was written
- The Founding Fathers wrote the Constitution

Question 9

- 1787

Question 10

- New York (Harbor)
- Liberty Island
- [Also acceptable are New Jersey, near New York City, and on the Hudson River.]

Civics Practice Test 9

Questions:

1. What are the two chambers that make up the US Congress?

2. What is the total number of senators in the US?

3. What is the final day that you are able to submit your applications for federal income tax?*

4. Why did the colonists engage in conflicts with the British?

5. The author of the Declaration of Independence is unknown.

6. Under what circumstances was the Declaration of Independence ratified?

7. Who were the people who lived in America before to the arrival of Europeans?

8. Which group of people were brought to the United States of America and sold into slavery?

9. When is the date that we celebrate the Fourth of July?*

10. Please name two national holidays that are celebrated in the US.

Answers:

Question 1

- The Senate (or upper house) and the House (or House of Representatives)

Question 2

- One hundred (100)

Question 3

- April 15

Question 4

- Because of high taxes (taxation without representation)
- Because the British army stayed in their houses (boarding, quartering)
- Because they didn't have self-government

Question 5

- (Thomas) Jefferson

Question 6

- July 4, 1776

Question 7

- American Indians
- Native Americans

Question 8

- Africans
- People from Africa

Question 9

- July 4

Question 10

- New Year's Day
- Martin Luther King, Jr. Day
- Presidents' Day
- Memorial Day
- Juneteenth
- Independence Day
- Labor Day
- Columbus Day
- Veterans Day
- Thanksgiving
- Christmas

Civics Practice Test 10

Questions:

1. For how many years do we elect a senator to serve in the United States Senate?

2. Who is now serving as a senator for your individual state?*

3. Which two political parties are considered to be the most influential in the US?*

4. As of right now, whose political party does the President belong to?

5. What is the current name of the person who serves as the Speaker of the House of Representatives?

6. In what time frame are all males required to register for the Selective Service?

7. What was one of the reasons that colonists migrated to the Americas?

8. What is the significance of the flag's thirteen stripes?

9. What is the reason for the flag's fifty stars?*

10. Can you tell me the name of the national anthem you sing?

Answers:

Question 1

- Six (6)

Question 2

- Responses may differ. If you reside in the District of Columbia or a US territory, indicate that D.C. (or the specific territory) does not have US Senators. To locate your state's US Senators, please visit senate.gov.

Question 3

- Democratic and Republican

Question 4

- Democratic (party)

Question 5

- Mike Johnson
- Johnson
- James Michael Johnson (birth name)
- (During a grace period ending 1 December, 2023) Patrick McHenry

Question 6

- At age eighteen (18)
- Between eighteen (18) and twenty-six (26)

Question 7

- Freedom
- Political liberty

- Religious freedom
- Economic opportunity
- Practice their religion
- Escape persecution

Question 8

- Because there were 13 original colonies
- Because the stripes represent the original colonies

Question 9

- Because there is one star for each state
- Because each star represents a state
- Because there are 50 states

Question 10

- The Star-Spangled Banner

CHAPTER 8

Enhanced Test Preparation Strategies

Becoming a US citizen is a significant goal, and achieving success in the naturalization process requires not only knowledge but also effective test preparation strategies. In this chapter, we will explore enhanced test preparation strategies, focusing on two crucial aspects: managing anxiety during the test and optimizing memorization and study time. These strategies are designed to empower individuals with the tools they need to approach the US citizenship test with confidence and success.

Managing Anxiety During the Test

Test anxiety is a common phenomenon that arises from the fear of failure, the pressure to perform, or concerns about meeting expectations. Recognizing the signs of test anxiety is the first step in addressing this challenge. Symptoms may include rapid heartbeat, shallow breathing, sweating, difficulty concentrating, and negative thoughts. By acknowledging these signs, individuals can take proactive steps to manage anxiety and optimize their performance during the naturalization test. Here are some strategies to help you navigate and mitigate anxiety, ensuring a more confident and successful naturalization experience.

1. **Practice Mindfulness Techniques:** Being completely immersed in the moment is an essential component of mindfulness, which enables one to concentrate on the work at hand and reduces feelings of anxiousness. Develop a habit of incorporating mindfulness practices into your everyday routine, such as meditation and activities that include deep breathing. You may find that engaging in these activities helps to calm your nerves and improves your capacity to remain present during the examination.

2. **Simulate Test Conditions:** Fear of the unknown can contribute to test anxiety. To alleviate this, familiarize yourself with the testing environment by simulating test conditions during your practice sessions. Use a timer, sit in a quiet space, and adhere to the same rules and regulations you'll encounter during the actual test. The more familiar you are with the testing conditions, the more confident and in control you'll feel.

3. **Positive Visualization:** Visualization is a powerful tool for managing anxiety. Take time to visualize yourself successfully navigating the test. Picture the testing room, recall your prepared answers, and imagine the sense of accomplishment after completing each section. Positive visualization can boost confidence, create a positive mindset, and reduce anxiety.

4. **Establish a Pre-Test Routine:** It is possible to send a signal to your brain that it is time to perform by developing a pre-test routine yourself. Whether it's a few moments of light exercise, listening to calming music, or reviewing a few key concepts, having a consistent routine can help you relax and focus before entering the testing environment.

5. **Stay Positive:** Maintain a positive mindset by reminding yourself of your accomplishments and the effort you've invested in preparing for the test. Positive affirmations can counteract negative thoughts and build confidence. Focus on the progress you've made and the knowledge you've acquired, reinforcing the idea that you are well-prepared for the naturalization test.

6. **Break Down the Test:** As an alternative to viewing the full test as an intimidating task, you should divide it up into pieces that are more doable. Focus on one question at a time, and approach the test as a series of smaller challenges. This approach can alleviate feelings of overwhelm and help you concentrate on each question without being distracted by the overall scope of the test.

7. **Seek Support:** Sharing your concerns and feelings with friends, family, or a support group can provide valuable perspective and encouragement. Discussing your anxieties allows you to express your emotions and receive support, reducing the sense of isolation that anxiety can bring. Knowing that others believe in your capabilities can boost your confidence.

8. **Use Relaxation Techniques:** Incorporate relaxation techniques into your routine to alleviate physical tension and promote a sense of calmness. Techniques such as progressive muscle relaxation or guided imagery can be particularly effective. Regular practice of these techniques can contribute to overall stress reduction and enhance your ability to manage anxiety during the test.

Optimizing Memorization and Study Time

Effective memorization and efficient use of study time are pivotal to mastering the required knowledge for the naturalization test. This section focuses on strategies to optimize memorization and study time, providing a comprehensive guide to enhance your preparation and increase your chances of success.

1. Create a Study Schedule

The foundation of effective study is a well-organized and realistic study schedule. Develop a plan that aligns with your daily routine, considering work, family commitments, and personal preferences. Set specific, achievable goals for each study session and allocate dedicated time for review. Consistency is key – maintaining a regular study schedule helps reinforce your understanding of the material over time.

Divide your study schedule into distinct phases, covering different subject areas or sections of the naturalization test. For example, focus on US history and government in one session and English language proficiency in another. This structured approach ensures a balanced and thorough preparation.

2. Utilize Active Learning Techniques

Engage in active learning to deepen your understanding and enhance memorization. Passive learning, such as simply reading or listening, is less effective than actively interacting with the material. Consider the following active learning techniques:

- **Summarization:** Summarize key concepts in your own words. This process reinforces your understanding and helps consolidate information.
- **Teaching:** Teach the material to someone else. Explaining concepts to others requires a comprehensive understanding, solidifying your knowledge.
- **Flashcards:** Create flashcards with questions on one side and answers on the other. This approach facilitates self-quizzing and promotes memory recall.

Active learning not only enhances your grasp of the material but also makes your study sessions more dynamic and engaging.

3. Implement the Spaced Repetition Technique

Leverage the spaced repetition technique to optimize memorization. This approach entails examining material at intervals that increase in frequency over the course of time. Instead of cramming all your study material at once, space out your review sessions. The spaced repetition technique promotes long-term retention, ensuring that you remember information more effectively by revisiting it at strategically spaced intervals.

Utilize flashcards or digital platforms that incorporate spaced repetition algorithms to tailor your study sessions based on your individual learning curve. This technique is particularly effective for memorizing dates, historical events, and other factual information.

4. Develop Mnemonic Devices

Mnemonic devices are memory aids that link complex information to easier-to-remember cues. Create acronyms, rhymes, or visual associations to help recall specific details. Mnemonic devices are especially useful for memorizing lists, sequences, or intricate information.

For example, to remember the names of the first ten amendments to the US Constitution, create a mnemonic using the first letter of each amendment: "B ill of R ights: F reedom of R eligion, F reedom of S peech, R ight to B ear A rms..."

5. Establish a Variety of Study Resources

Diversify your study resources to cater to different learning styles and preferences. Combine traditional textbooks, online resources, videos, and interactive tools to reinforce your understanding from various perspectives. The use of multimedia resources can make your study sessions more engaging and effective.

Explore reputable online platforms, such as official government websites, educational videos, and interactive quizzes, to complement your primary study materials. The diverse formats will cater to different aspects of your learning, enhancing comprehension and retention.

6. Practice Regularly with Mock Tests

Incorporate regular practice tests into your study routine. Mock tests simulate the conditions of the actual naturalization test, providing a valuable opportunity to assess your knowledge and familiarize yourself with the test format. Benefits of incorporating mock tests into your study plan include:

- **Identifying Weak Areas:** Mock tests reveal areas where you may need additional focus or review.
- **Improving Time Management:** Through the use of practice exams, you may improve your time management skills and ensure that you devote an adequate amount of time to each area.
- **Building Confidence:** Successfully completing practice tests boosts confidence and reduces anxiety about the actual test.

Use official practice materials provided by USCIS to ensure accuracy and alignment with the content of the naturalization test.

7. Focus on Weak Areas

Identify your weaker areas based on practice tests and allocate additional study time to reinforce those specific concepts. Prioritize your efforts based on areas that contribute significantly to the overall test content. By addressing weaknesses early in your preparation, you build a solid foundation and increase your overall confidence.

Use the feedback from practice tests to guide your study sessions. If certain questions consistently pose challenges, delve deeper into those topics. A targeted and strategic approach ensures that you maximize the effectiveness of your study time.

8. Create a Visual Study Aid

Visual aids can enhance memorization and serve as quick reference tools during your final review. Develop a visual study aid, such as a mind map or concept chart, to organize information visually. This visual representation helps you see the connections between different concepts and reinforces the structure of your knowledge.

Use colors, diagrams, and images to make your visual study aid more engaging and memorable. The act of creating the visual aid itself contributes to your understanding and retention of the material.

9. Join Study Groups

Consider joining a study group to complement your individual study efforts. Study groups provide an opportunity to discuss concepts with peers, share insights, and benefit from diverse perspectives. Engaging in group discussions helps reinforce your understanding of the material through active participation and collaboration.

Choose study group members who are committed to the preparation process and have a positive and collaborative mindset. Share your strengths and learn from others, creating a supportive environment for mutual growth.

10.Take Breaks

While maintaining a consistent study schedule is crucial, incorporating short breaks into your study sessions is equally important. Breaks help prevent burnout and maintain your focus and concentration. Use this time to stretch, take a short walk, or engage in a different activity to refresh your mind.

There is a well-known strategy for managing one's time called the Pomodoro Technique. This technique entails working in concentrated intervals of 25 minutes, followed by a brief break. You should try out a variety of intervals over time to determine which one is best for you, making sure that breaks lead to higher production.

11.Evaluate Your Study Techniques

Regularly assess the effectiveness of your study techniques and be open to adjusting your approach. If certain methods prove less productive, explore alternative strategies to keep your study sessions dynamic and engaging. Experiment with different approaches to determine what resonates most with your learning style.

Consider seeking feedback from study group members or mentors who can provide insights into your study habits. A willingness to adapt and refine your study techniques ensures continuous improvement throughout your preparation.

12. Set Realistic Goals

Set realistic, achievable goals for each study session. Break down your study plan into smaller tasks, making it easier to track your progress and maintain motivation. Celebrate small victories along the way, acknowledging the effort you put into each study session. Setting realistic goals contributes to a positive mindset and reinforces your commitment to the naturalization preparation process.

CHAPTER

Avoiding Common Pitfalls

9

Embarking on the journey towards US citizenship is a significant undertaking, and navigating the naturalization process requires careful attention to detail. In this chapter, we will explore common pitfalls that applicants may encounter and provide guidance on how to avoid them.

Top Reasons for Application Denial and How to Avoid Them

1. Incomplete or Inaccurate Application

One of the primary reasons for application denial stems from incomplete or inaccurately filled-out forms. The N-400 application demands meticulous attention to detail, and any missing information or errors can lead to complications in the naturalization process.

Avoidance Strategy: To overcome this hurdle, applicants must conduct a thorough review of the N-400 application before submission. This review process should include checking for completeness, accuracy, and consistency in the provided information. Seeking assistance from legal professionals or utilizing resources provided by USCIS can further enhance an applicant's understanding of the application requirements. Taking the time to ensure that all fields are accurately and completely filled out is an investment in the success of the naturalization journey.

2. Failure to Meet Residency Requirements

Meeting the continuous residence and physical presence requirements is fundamental to the naturalization process. Failing to maintain a permanent residence in the US for the required period can be a major roadblock to citizenship.

Avoidance Strategy: To avoid this pitfall, applicants should remain vigilant about meeting the continuous residence and physical presence requirements. Keeping detailed records of travels, addresses, and any extended stays outside the US is crucial for maintaining compliance. Maintaining a permanent residence in the country throughout the stipulated period demonstrates commitment to the requirements and positions the applicant for a successful naturalization application.

3. Lack of Good Moral Character

Upholding good moral character is a cornerstone of eligibility for US citizenship. Engaging in criminal activities, failing to pay taxes, or violating US laws can jeopardize an applicant's moral character and lead to denial.

Avoidance Strategy: To avoid this potential pitfall, applicants should prioritize ethical behavior and compliance with US laws. Addressing any legal issues promptly and consulting with an immigration attorney if there are concerns about moral character can be instrumental in navigating this aspect of the application process. Demonstrating a commitment to lawful conduct and societal values strengthens an applicant's case for naturalization.

4. Failure to Pass the English or Civics Test

The English language proficiency test and civics test are integral components of the naturalization process. Failing to demonstrate the required proficiency in English or civics knowledge can result in denial.

Avoidance Strategy: Comprehensive preparation for the English language and civics tests is key to avoiding this obstacle. Utilizing study materials provided by USCIS, regular practice, and participation in study groups can significantly enhance an applicant's knowledge and readiness. Familiarity with the test formats and targeted preparation in areas of weakness contribute to a successful outcome in these crucial components of the naturalization process.

5. Failing to Attend Biometrics Appointment or Interview

Timely attendance at biometrics appointments and interviews is crucial for a smooth naturalization process. Failure to appear as scheduled can result in complications and may lead to denial.

Avoidance Strategy: To avoid this pitfall, applicants must mark all important dates on their calendars and prioritize attendance at biometrics appointments and interviews. In cases where conflicts or issues may arise, prompt communication with USCIS to reschedule and explain any impediments is essential. Prioritizing attendance underscores an applicant's commitment to the naturalization process.

6. Unlawful Presence in the US

Accumulating unlawful presence in the US, such as overstaying visas or violating immigration laws, can be a significant barrier to naturalization.

Avoidance Strategy: Adherence to US immigration laws is critical to avoiding unlawful presence. Seeking legal advice if there are concerns about immigration status and addressing potential issues before applying for naturalization can prevent complications. A clean immigration record is fundamental for a successful naturalization application.

7. Financial Issues

Outstanding financial obligations, including unpaid taxes or child support, can impact an applicant's eligibility for US citizenship.

Avoidance Strategy: Staying current on financial obligations such as taxes and child support payments is paramount. Addressing any outstanding debts and consulting with a financial advisor if needed demonstrates financial responsibility and enhances an applicant's chances of a favorable naturalization outcome.

8. Failure to Register for Selective Service (Males Only)

Eligible males are required to register for Selective Service, and failure to do so can lead to denial of naturalization.

Avoidance Strategy: Ensuring that eligible males register for Selective Service before the age of 26 is crucial. This requirement is applicable to most males between the ages of 18 and 25. Failing to register can result in disqualification from US citizenship, making timely registration imperative.

9. Misrepresentation or Fraud

Providing false or misleading information during the application process is a serious offense that can lead to denial and legal consequences.

Avoidance Strategy: Honesty throughout the application process is paramount. Providing truthful and accurate information ensures credibility and trust in the eyes of USCIS. Misrepresentation or fraud can lead to severe consequences, including denial of citizenship and potential legal action. Upholding integrity throughout the application process is not only a legal requirement but a reflection of an applicant's commitment to the values of US citizenship.

Mistakes to Avoid at Interviews

1. Lack of Preparation

Mistake: One of the most common errors is arriving at the interview underprepared. Lack of preparation can manifest in various ways, from not being familiar with the questions that may be asked to failing to review one's own application thoroughly.

Avoidance Strategy: Preparation is key to a successful interview. Applicants should thoroughly review their application, paying attention to details such as dates, addresses, and other personal information. Equally important is studying the provided materials, including the US Constitution, the Bill of Rights, and other relevant documents. Practicing potential interview questions with a friend or family member can also help build confidence and readiness for the actual interview.

2. Failure to Understand Questions

Mistake: Misunderstanding questions during the interview can lead to providing inaccurate or incomplete answers. This may happen due to nervousness or a lack of clarity about the question being asked.

Avoidance Strategy: Listening carefully and ensuring a clear understanding of each question is critical. If an applicant is uncertain about the meaning of a question, it is perfectly acceptable to ask the interviewer for clarification. Providing thoughtful and accurate answers requires a clear comprehension of the questions posed, and seeking clarification demonstrates a commitment to accuracy.

3. Forgetting Your Original Documents on the Day of the Interview

Presenting all necessary documents to support the information provided during the application is crucial during the interview. Failure to bring essential documents may leave a negative impression on the officer and could potentially lead to application rejection.

Avoidance Strategy: To avoid this mistake, ensure that you have all required documents with you on the day of the interview. This includes your interview appointment notice, Form I-551 (Permanent Resident Card), state-issued identification (such as a driver's license), and all valid and expired passports and travel documents documenting your absences from the US since becoming a permanent resident. Review the USCIS document checklist (Form M-477) for additional documents that may be required. By thoroughly preparing and organizing your documents in advance, you can demonstrate your readiness and attention to detail to the interviewing officer.

4. Inappropriate Dressing

Your appearance during the interview is an important aspect of making a positive impression on the interviewing officer. Inappropriate attire can detract from your professionalism and may reflect poorly on your candidacy for citizenship.

Avoidance Strategy: On the day of the interview, dress in formal attire to convey professionalism and respect for the process. Avoid wearing clothing items such as jeans, shorts, sweatpants, tank tops, flip-flops, or T-shirts with inappropriate printings. Instead, opt for comfortable yet formal attire, such as business casual or formal attire. Choose clothing that is clean, neat, and free of distracting or offensive graphics. By dressing appropriately for the occasion, you demonstrate your seriousness and readiness for US citizenship.

5. Overconfidence or Nervousness

Mistake: Finding the right balance between confidence and humility is essential during the interview. Applicants may either come across as overly confident, potentially appearing arrogant, or display excessive nervousness, which can impact the quality of their responses.

Avoidance Strategy: Strike a balance between confidence and humility. Confidence should be grounded in preparation and a genuine understanding of the material. Engaging in mock interviews, practicing relaxation techniques, and visualizing a positive interview experience can help manage nervousness. A poised and self-assured demeanor contributes to a positive impression on the interviewer.

6. Inconsistencies with Application

Mistake: Providing inconsistent information during the interview compared to what was submitted in the application can raise concerns and may lead to further scrutiny.

Avoidance Strategy: Consistency is crucial. Applicants should ensure that their answers align with the information provided in their application. Reviewing the application before the interview can help refresh the memory and prevent inadvertent inconsistencies. If there have been changes or updates since the application submission, applicants should be prepared to explain them clearly and transparently.

7. Inability to Speak or Understand English

Mistake: The ability to speak and understand English is a fundamental requirement for US citizenship. Inability to communicate effectively in English can result in a denial of the application.

Avoidance Strategy: Prioritizing English language proficiency is vital. Regular practice in speaking, listening, and comprehending English is essential for a successful interview. Engaging in conversational English, watching English-language media, and participating in language exchange programs can contribute to enhanced proficiency. Language preparation should be ongoing, not just limited to the period leading up to the interview.

8. Failure to Bring Required Documents

Mistake: Not bringing all required documents to the interview, including the green card, travel documents, and any additional evidence requested by USCIS, can lead to delays and complications.

Avoidance Strategy: Organization is key. Applicants should compile all required documents well in advance of the interview and bring them in an organized manner. A checklist can be useful in ensuring that all necessary paperwork is accounted for. Being proactive in gathering and presenting the required documents demonstrates preparedness and responsibility.

9. Unauthorized Assistance from Representatives

Mistake: Having unauthorized individuals, such as friends or family members, providing assistance during the interview is a common mistake. Only legal representatives authorized by USCIS should accompany applicants.

Avoidance Strategy: Applicants should attend the interview alone unless they have a legal representative authorized to accompany them. Unauthorized representatives can lead to complications, and it is crucial to adhere to USCIS guidelines regarding who may be present during the interview.

In addition to avoiding these common mistakes, it is important for applicants to approach the interview with a positive and respectful attitude. Demonstrating genuine enthusiasm for becoming a US citizen and expressing gratitude for the opportunity can leave a positive impression on the interviewer. Additionally, maintaining a professional demeanor and adhering to any specific guidelines provided by USCIS contribute to a smooth and successful interview experience.

Correcting Mistakes in N-400 Application

The N-400 application serves as a comprehensive record of an applicant's personal information, immigration history, and eligibility for US citizenship. Accurate and truthful completion of the application is paramount, as any discrepancies or mistakes may impact the outcome of the naturalization process. Recognizing the significance of accuracy in the application is the first step toward a successful correction process.

Types of Mistakes and Common Errors

Before delving into the correction process, it is essential to identify the types of mistakes that can occur in the N-400 application. Common errors may include:

10. **Typographical Errors:** Simple mistakes such as misspelled names, incorrect dates, or transposed numbers.

11. **Incomplete Information:** Failure to provide all required information in the designated sections of the application.

12. **Outdated Information:** Changes in personal circumstances, addresses, or other details that have occurred since the application was submitted.

13. **Misinterpretation of Questions:** Providing answers that may be interpreted differently than intended due to a misunderstanding of the question.

14. **Omissions:** Failing to include relevant details or documentation as required by USCIS.

Step-by-Step Guide to Correcting Mistakes

Correcting mistakes in the N-400 application involves a systematic approach to ensure accuracy and completeness. The following step-by-step guide provides a structured framework for applicants to navigate the correction process effectively:

1. **Review Your Application Thoroughly:** Before initiating any corrections, carefully review your entire N-400 application. Take note of any areas where mistakes or discrepancies may exist, including typographical errors, missing information, or outdated details.

2. **Identify the Nature of the Mistakes:** Categorize the mistakes based on their nature. Distinguish between typographical errors, factual inaccuracies, and areas where additional information or documentation is required.

3. **Gather Supporting Documents:** For factual inaccuracies or omissions, gather any supporting documents that may be necessary to rectify the mistakes. This may include updated residency information, legal documents, or any other relevant records.

4. **Download and Complete Form N-400, Part 2:** To correct mistakes on your application, you will need to download and complete Form N-400, Part 2, officially titled the "Application for Naturalization." This form is specifically designed for addressing changes or corrections to your application.

5. **Complete the Form Accurately:** When completing Form N-400, Part 2, provide accurate and updated information. Clearly indicate the sections that require correction and provide the correct details. Be thorough and meticulous in your responses.

6. **Attach a Cover Letter:** Include a cover letter with your corrected form. The cover letter should concisely explain the nature of the mistakes, provide the correct information, and express your commitment to ensuring accuracy in your application.

7. **Submit Supporting Documents:** If your corrections require supporting documents, ensure that you include these along with your corrected form and cover letter. This may include updated residency proofs, legal documents, or any other relevant records.

8. **Submit the Corrections to USCIS:** Mail the corrected Form N-400, Part 2, along with the cover letter and supporting documents, to the appropriate USCIS address. Ensure that you retain a copy of the corrected form, cover letter, and any submitted documents for your records.

9. **Follow Up on Your Submission:** After submitting the corrections, it is advisable to follow up with USCIS to confirm the receipt of your corrected materials. You may use the USCIS case status online tool or contact USCIS through the provided channels to inquire about the status of your correction.

10. **Be Prepared for Additional Requests:** In some cases, USCIS may request additional information or documentation to process your corrections. Be prepared to promptly respond to any such requests to avoid delays in the naturalization process.

Common Mistakes and How to Correct Them:

To provide a more practical understanding, let's explore specific scenarios of common mistakes and how applicants can effectively correct them:

Scenario 1: Typographical Errors

Common Mistake: Misspelled names, incorrect dates, or transposed numbers.

Correction Process:

- Download Form N-400, Part 2.
- Complete the form with the correct spelling or numerical information.
- Attach a cover letter explaining the nature of the typographical errors and providing the correct details.
- Submit the corrected form and cover letter to USCIS.

Scenario 2: Change of Address

Common Mistake: Failure to update a change of address since submitting the application.

Correction Process:

- Download Form N-400, Part 2.
- Complete the form with the updated address information.
- Attach a cover letter explaining the change of address and providing the correct details.
- Submit the corrected form and cover letter to USCIS.

Scenario 3: Misinterpretation of Questions

Common Mistake: Providing answers that may be interpreted differently due to a misunderstanding of the question.

Correction Process:

- Download Form N-400, Part 2.

- Review the questions carefully and provide accurate responses.
- Attach a cover letter explaining any areas of potential misunderstanding and providing clarified responses.
- Submit the corrected form and cover letter to USCIS.

Scenario 4: Failure to Include Relevant Documents

Common Mistake: Omitting required documents, such as updated residency proofs or legal records.

Correction Process:

- Download Form N-400, Part 2.
- Complete the form with the correct information.
- Gather the omitted documents and include them with the corrected form.
- Attach a cover letter explaining the omission and providing the correct details.
- Submit the corrected form, cover letter, and supporting documents to USCIS.

Scenario 5: Outdated Information

Common Mistake: Failing to update personal information, such as marital status or employment details.

Correction Process:

- Download Form N-400, Part 2.
- Complete the form with the updated information.
- Attach a cover letter explaining the changes and providing the correct details.
- Submit the corrected form and cover letter to USCIS.

Factors That Can Disqualify from US Citizenship

1. Criminal Convictions and Moral Character

A fundamental requirement for US citizenship is possessing good moral character. Criminal convictions, especially those involving serious offenses such as felonies, can raise concerns about an applicant's moral character. Individuals with a history of criminal activity may find their naturalization application denied.

Mitigation Strategy: If an applicant has a criminal history, it is crucial to consult with an immigration attorney to assess the impact on their naturalization eligibility. In some cases, rehabilitation, completion of probation or parole, and evidence of a reformed lifestyle can be presented to demonstrate an improvement in moral character.

2. Failure to Pay Taxes

Compliance with tax laws is a significant aspect of US citizenship eligibility. Failure to file tax returns or outstanding tax liabilities can be viewed as a lack of financial responsibility, potentially leading to disqualification.

Mitigation Strategy: Address any outstanding tax issues promptly. Pay any owed taxes and work with tax professionals to ensure compliance with tax laws. Providing evidence of tax compliance and rectifying any financial discrepancies can contribute to a positive assessment of an applicant's eligibility.

3. Unlawful Presence and Immigration Violations

Accumulating unlawful presence in the US, overstaying visas, or violating immigration laws can be grounds for denial of naturalization. Maintaining lawful status and adhering to immigration regulations are vital for a successful naturalization journey.

Mitigation Strategy: Seek legal advice if there are concerns about immigration status or potential violations. Clearing up any immigration issues, obtaining legal status, and demonstrating adherence to US immigration laws are crucial steps to mitigate the impact of unlawful presence on naturalization eligibility.

4. Failure to Register for Selective Service

Male applicants between the ages of 18 and 25 are required to register for Selective Service. Failure to register can result in disqualification from US citizenship.

Mitigation Strategy: Ensure timely registration for Selective Service before the age of 26. If an applicant failed to register due to an oversight, they should promptly register and provide documentation of their registration status during the naturalization process.

5. Fraudulent Activities and Misrepresentation

Providing false or misleading information during the naturalization process is a serious offense that can lead to denial of US citizenship. Fraudulent activities, including misrepresentation of facts, can have severe consequences.

Mitigation Strategy: Honesty is paramount. Applicants should provide truthful and accurate information throughout the naturalization process. If there are concerns about prior misrepresentations, consulting with an immigration attorney to address and rectify these issues is essential.

6. National Security Concerns

Engaging in activities that raise national security concerns can lead to disqualification from US citizenship. This includes affiliations with organizations or actions that may be deemed a threat to national security.

Mitigation Strategy: Avoid involvement in activities that may raise national security concerns. Applicants should be cautious about affiliations and actions that could be perceived as jeopardizing national security and seek legal advice if uncertain about any potential issues.

7. Failing the English or Civics Test

Demonstrating proficiency in the English language and knowledge of US civics is a requirement for naturalization. Failing either of these tests during the naturalization interview can lead to denial.

Mitigation Strategy: Prioritize comprehensive preparation for the English language and civics tests. Utilize study materials provided by USCIS, engage in language practice, and participate in civics education programs to enhance proficiency in these areas.

8. Continuous Residence and Physical Presence Requirements

Applicants must meet specific continuous residence and physical presence requirements to qualify for US citizenship. Failure to maintain a permanent residence in the US throughout the required period can lead to disqualification.

Mitigation Strategy: Plan and document travels carefully to ensure compliance with continuous residence and physical presence requirements. Maintaining a permanent residence in the US and avoiding prolonged absences is essential for meeting these criteria.

9. Defaulting on Child Support Payments

Outstanding child support payments can impact an applicant's eligibility for US citizenship, reflecting on their financial responsibility and moral character.

Mitigation Strategy: Stay current on child support payments and address any outstanding obligations. Demonstrating financial responsibility and compliance with legal obligations contributes to a positive assessment of an applicant's eligibility.

10. Health-Related Inadmissibility

Certain health-related issues may render an individual inadmissible for US citizenship. This includes communicable diseases of public health significance.

Mitigation Strategy: Consult with immigration and healthcare professionals to address health-related concerns. Providing medical documentation, obtaining necessary vaccinations, and addressing health issues in a timely manner can mitigate health-related inadmissibility concerns.

Navigating the naturalization process requires a comprehensive understanding of potential factors that can disqualify an individual from US citizenship. By being aware of these factors and implementing mitigation strategies, applicants can proactively address concerns and increase their chances of a successful naturalization journey.

Thank you immensely for reaching this point.

Dear Reader,

Our team has invested significant time and effort into crafting this book, aiming to deliver a work of quality and insight.

A review from you would not only be incredibly appreciated but also instrumental in helping us share our material with a wider audience.

We are profoundly grateful for your support and sincerely thank you for any feedback you choose to provide!

Conclusion and Additional Resources

Final Thoughts and Encouragement

As we reach the conclusion of this comprehensive US Citizenship Study Guide, it's important to reflect on the journey that lies ahead for those seeking to become proud citizens of the US. The path to citizenship is not merely a bureaucratic process; it is a transformative journey that embodies the values of dedication, perseverance, and commitment to the principles upon which this great nation was founded.

Final Thoughts on the Journey to Citizenship

Becoming a US citizen is a significant milestone in the lives of individuals from diverse backgrounds and walks of life. It represents not only a legal status but also a profound connection to the ideals of democracy, freedom, and opportunity that define the American experience. As you embark on this journey, remember that citizenship is more than just a title; it is a privilege and a responsibility that comes with rights and duties.

Throughout this study guide, we have explored various aspects of the naturalization process, from eligibility requirements to test preparation strategies to common pitfalls to avoid. We have provided detailed insights, practical tips, and valuable resources to support you on your path to citizenship. However, beyond the technicalities of the naturalization process, it is essential to recognize the deeper significance of citizenship and the values it represents.

Encouragement for the Journey Ahead

As you navigate the naturalization process, remember that you are not alone. Countless immigrants who came before you embarked on this journey and achieved US citizenship, contributing their diverse talents, cultures, and perspectives to enrich American society. Draw inspiration from their stories of resilience, determination, and triumph over adversity.

Embrace the opportunity to learn about the history, values, and institutions of the US. Engage with the communities around you, participate in civic activities, and contribute to the betterment of society. Citizenship is not just a legal status; it is a commitment to active participation in the democratic process, to upholding the rule of law, and to promoting the common good.

Stay resilient in the face of challenges and setbacks. The naturalization process may present obstacles and uncertainties, but perseverance and determination will carry you through. Seek support from family, friends, and community organizations. Utilize the resources and assistance available to you, including legal services, educational programs, and citizenship workshops.

Approach the naturalization interview with confidence, preparedness, and respect. Remember to listen carefully, respond thoughtfully, and present yourself with professionalism and courtesy. Demonstrate your commitment to becoming an informed and engaged citizen who values the rights and responsibilities of citizenship.

Above all, cherish the privilege of becoming a citizen of the US. Recognize the opportunities that citizenship affords you – the right to vote, the ability to travel freely, the opportunity to pursue your dreams, and the assurance of protection under the law. But also, embrace the responsibilities that come with citizenship – the duty to uphold the Constitution, to respect the rights of others, and to contribute positively to society.

As you embark on this journey to US citizenship, remember that you are part of a vibrant and diverse tapestry of individuals who share a common aspiration for a better future. Your journey reflects the enduring spirit of America – a nation built by immigrants, strengthened by diversity, and united by a shared commitment to liberty and justice for all.

In closing, we extend our best wishes to all aspiring citizens as you embark on this transformative journey. May your path to citizenship be filled with hope, courage, and success. Embrace the values of democracy, liberty, and equality that define the American identity. And may your journey to citizenship be a testament to the enduring promise of America – a land of opportunity, a beacon of freedom, and a home for all who seek a better life.

References and Credits

1. Explanations of procedures and timelines

Explanations regarding examination procedures and timelines faithfully reproduce what is reported in this regard on the official USCIS website.

https://www.uscis.gov/

2. Writing Vocabulary List

The Writing Vocabulary List image is from the official USCIS website

https://www.uscis.gov/sites/default/files/document/guides/writing_vocab.pdf

3. Reading Vocabulary List

The Reading Vocabulary List image is from the official USCIS website

https://www.uscis.gov/sites/default/files/document/guides/reading_vocab.pdf

4. Civics Test Questions

All 100 civics test questions were taken from the official USCIS website

https://www.uscis.gov/sites/default/files/document/questions-and-answers/100q.pdf

Made in the USA
Middletown, DE
10 September 2024

60714980R00060